All truths are easy to understand once they are discovered; the point is to discover them.

—*Galileo Galilei*

CRYSTAL ZODIAC

AN ASTROLOGICAL GUIDE TO ENHANCING YOUR LIFE WITH CRYSTALS

KATIE HUANG

FOUNDER OF ☽ LOVE BY LUNA

HOUGHTON MIFFLIN HARCOURT
BOSTON NEW YORK 2020

For information about permission to reproduce selections from this book, write to trade.permissions@hmhco.com or to Permissions, Houghton Mifflin Harcourt Publishing Company, 3 Park Avenue, 19th Floor, New York, New York 10016.

hmhbooks.com

Library of Congress Cataloging-in-Publication Data
Names: Huang, Katie, author.
Title: Crystal zodiac : an astrological guide to enhancing
your life with crystals / Katie Huang, founder of love by Luna.
Description: Boston : Houghton Mifflin Harcourt, 2020.
Identifiers: LCCN 2019045715 (print) | LCCN 2019045716 (ebook) |
ISBN 9780358213048 (hardback) | ISBN 9780358310266 | ISBN 9780358310341 |
ISBN 9780358213369 (ebook)
Subjects: LCSH: Crystals—Miscellanea. | Astrology.
Classification: LCC BF1442.C78 H83 2020 (print) | LCC BF1442.C78 (ebook) | DDC 133/.2548—dc23
LC record available at https://lccn.loc.gov/2019045715
LC ebook record available at https://lccn.loc.gov/2019045716

Cover design by Eleanor Kwei
Interior design by Rachel Marek
Cover and endsheets photography by Micah Schmidt

Printed in China

SCP 10 9 8 7 6 5 4 3 2 1

CONTENTS

NOT JUST FOR MYSTICS

When the people of ancient civilizations looked up at the night sky they found stories and guidance in the stars, and they grouped together in constellations the celestial bodies that appeared to form images. Though the names of the zodiac's constellations have mythical origins, the patterns themselves served a number of practical purposes throughout history. The position of the stars helped explorers successfully navigate the globe and assisted farmers by attuning them to the cycles of the seasons. Ultimately, the recognizable patterns of the constellations enabled people to become more aware of their surroundings and better orient themselves in a changing world.

Today, we use astrology and crystals as tools of mindfulness that encourage a similar sense of consciousness about where we are and where we want to go—and, as with constellations, we don't need to be mystical, magical, or spiritually inclined in order to use them. While these tools have sometimes been linked with science or religion, astrology and crystals are simply a means of self-reflection that provide an opportunity for self-discovery, personal growth, and emotional development. By offering an objective understanding of our character as well as insights into our past cycles and current behaviors, these tools heighten our receptivity and guide us toward meaningful and practical changes that will improve our quality of life. When we use the two in tandem, we can begin to weave mindfulness practices into our day-to-day rhythms and move joyfully toward our full potential.

Wellness for You

What is wellness, anyway? The term is used so broadly it can be hard to define, let alone determine how to form your own wellness practices. Technically, wellness is simply a state of complete physical, mental, and social well-being—but it's about more than maintaining balance. Wellness is an active process and a way of life in which healthy and fulfilling choices are made daily through awareness, intention, and deliberate action.

The foundation of wellness is built upon the relationship with the self, and, like fitness and nutrition, wellness practice is not one-size-fits-all. There's a reason your friend swears by yoga but you find it hard to concentrate while on the mat, and why you love solitude but others find alone time stressful. The best way to nurture the connection between your mind and body will depend on your temperament, goals, and needs.

Crystals and Constellations

Cultivating self-awareness sounds simple, but leading a conscious life requires sustained effort and practice. When we're juggling work, family, and relationships, being tuned in to our thoughts and deliberate in our actions can be difficult—and aligning the two even more challenging. Astrology and crystals are powerful tools for introspection and change because they bridge the gap between our thoughts and actions. While our personal astrology provides insight into our behaviors and patterns, crystals prompt us to act on these insights by grounding our intentions in the physical world.

On your wellness journey, think of astrology as your road map and crystals as your vehicle. Either one, used on its own, can help you reach your destination. When used together, however, these two forces render your path much clearer. The biggest benefit of using astrology and crystals in tandem is that they help you craft a more personalized approach to wellness, outlining mindfulness practices and self-care routines that are tailor made for you.

ASTROLOGY OVERVIEW

A strology isn't the answer, it poses the question. A common misconception about astrology is that it acts like a Magic 8 Ball, predicting the future or describing one's personality in absolutes. But no system can completely define who you are because who you are is constantly evolving, changing with each new experience and person you meet. While specific traits and habits are linked to certain signs, these correlations are soft guidelines rather than hard rules. Astrology's function is to encourage us to think about who we are, not to tell us who we are. When we ask ourselves if we see a sign's tendencies reflected in our behavior and actions—or in those of our loved ones—we not only become more conscious of the ways in which we interact with the world, we better understand, empathize, and relate to those around us.

The Elements and Qualities of Astrology

The twelve signs that comprise the zodiac each bring a unique light to the world. However, signs that share the same element or quality possess certain similarities, as both factors influence a sign's general temperament. The four elements—fire, earth, air, and water—reveal a sign's basic tendencies, while the three qualities, or "modalities"—cardinal, fixed, and mutable—indicate a sign's approach to life. Recognizing the distinctions between the elements and qualities, and their combined effects, can highlight the strengths, weaknesses, and potential compatibility of different signs.

Elements

FIRE SIGNS

ARIES
LEO
SAGITTARIUS

bold, spontaneous, confident, passionate, enthusiastic, unafraid of risk

EARTH SIGNS

TAURUS
VIRGO
CAPRICORN

responsible, trustworthy, down to earth, attracted to stability and security

AIR SIGNS

GEMINI
LIBRA
AQUARIUS

free thinking, curious, social, welcoming of change, open to new opportunities for learning

WATER SIGNS

CANCER
SCORPIO
PISCES

sensitive, emotionally deep, intuitive, empathetic, drawn to nurturing, protecting, and healing

Qualities

CARDINAL SIGNS

ARIES
CANCER
LIBRA
CAPRICORN

self-starting, pioneering, enterprising, constantly moving forward and taking action

FIXED SIGNS

TAURUS
LEO
SCORPIO
AQUARIUS

determined, stable, deliberative, focused, concerned with sustaining their environment

MUTABLE SIGNS

GEMINI
VIRGO
SAGITTARIUS
PISCES

flexible, impressionable, highly adaptable, able to navigate a variety of circumstances and transitions

You're More Than Your Sun Sign

When people say, "What's your sign?" they are most likely asking about your sun sign, which is determined by your date of birth. With its central position, the sun represents the core of who we are—our inner essence shining for the world to see. Yet, as big an effect as the sun has on our personality, it is still only one piece of the larger cosmic puzzle of our identity. If you've noticed that your two Leo friends seem nothing alike, this is why! Their sun sign may be the same, but it represents a broad stroke of their personalities rather than a complete picture.

Just as the sun illuminates one dimension of who we are, each of the planets (by tradition, the moon and sun count as planets in astrology) sheds light on a different part of our psyche—from the way we process emotions to our communication style and even our approach to love. To learn the signs in which your planets fall, you must first calculate your natal chart (see "Finding Your Natal Chart" on page 10).

By understanding that our personality is multifaceted, charged with the energy of multiple signs, we can begin to peel back the individual layers of our thoughts and behaviors and gain a clearer perspective on how these energies operate separately as well as how they coalesce.

The Planets and Their Meaning

In astrology, each of the planets represents a different area of life or energy. The area of the sky (the zodiac sign) where a planet is positioned affects the way its energy is expressed. The planet's signature area—for example, love or communication—is colored by the traits of that sign.

The Big Three

The two luminaries (sun and moon), plus the ascendant, are considered the "Big Three" of astrology, the main astrological points that relay the most significant information about your natal chart. These points have the greatest impact on your personality, and provide an accurate snapshot of your larger astrological profile. Developing an understanding of your sun, moon, and ascendant combination will reveal what you want (sun), what you need (moon), and how you go about getting it (ascendant).

The **sun** represents the core of your identity, and remains constant throughout life. It's the fundamental sense of self that informs your basic nature, personality, ego, will, and purpose.

The **moon** represents your inner self and emotional foundation. It indicates the way you process feelings, your instinctive responses to the

Finding Your Natal Chart

A natal chart, or "birth chart," is an astrological blueprint of where the planets were located in the sky at the exact moment you were born—it is calculated using the date, time, and location of your birth. With such precise information, it's unlikely that many people share your natal chart, which is what makes astrology so special—the insights are highly specific to you!

To calculate your natal chart, input your birth info into any of the free natal chart calculators easily found online, or consult an astrologer for help. If you don't know your exact time of birth, make your best estimate or simply enter noon. While you won't be able to accurately determine all your planetary placements without your birth time, you can learn the majority of them with just your birth date.

world around you, and what makes you feel comfortable, nurtured, and secure. Because the moon is a more guarded, private planet, only those closest to you will be able to pick up on your moon sign traits.

The **ascendant**, or rising sign, is the sign that was rising on the eastern horizon at the exact moment you were born. Though technically not a planet, this placement has a profound effect on the way you interact with others and how they perceive you. People often mistake your ascendant for your sun sign, since it represents your outermost self. As the image you project into the world, your ascendant is the first impression you make, the mask you wear when meeting new people.

The Inner Planets

In addition to the sun and moon (which also fall into this group), the "faster"-moving planets—Mercury, Venus, and Mars—are known as the inner planets, or personal planets. These planets travel quickly through the entire zodiac and define your individual identity. While the Big Three characterize the core aspects of your personality, the remaining personal planets shape your day-to-day behaviors and interactions with others in areas such as communication or relationships.

Mercury represents your communication style and way of thinking. It indicates how you express yourself, the way you process and organize information, and your approach to learning.

Venus represents your values in love and romantic relationships. It demonstrates how you give and receive love, what you desire in a partner, who you attract and how, and your personal aesthetic and sense of beauty.

Mars represents your primal drive, aggressive instincts, and initiative. It reveals what spurs you to action, how you handle conflict, your ability to take risks, and what attracts you sexually.

The Outer Planets

The outer planets move slowly through the signs of the zodiac, sometimes taking fifteen years to complete a single transit. As a result, these planets shape generations more than individuals. Because these planets represent external influences with indirect effects, they usually indicate social and cultural transformations that play out over time rather than ones resulting from personal choices. However, the placements of your outer planets can point to the broader, collective themes you may encounter in your life.

Jupiter represents the larger life philosophies you live by, higher learning, and expansion.

Saturn exemplifies the challenges in life that make you grow, as well as your relationship to structure.

Uranus embodies revolution, sudden change, and the pursuit of freedom.

Neptune represents transcendence, illusion, and inspiration.

Pluto denotes the subconscious, creative destruction, power struggles, and transformation.

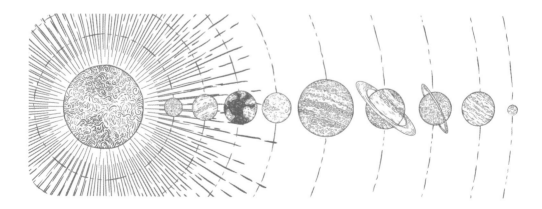

Planet Rulerships and States

The energy of each planet blends differently with the energy of each sign, resulting in various levels of compatibility between them. Each sign has a "ruling planet," which describes an affinity between a planet and a sign. A ruling planet exerts more influence over a given sign than any other planet, and feels at ease when positioned in the sign it rules. Depending on a planet's relationship to a sign, the planet can inhabit a special state, or "dignity," that varies in comfort level, strength, and ease of expression. The most commonly used of the traditional essential dignities are: domicile, exaltation, detriment, and fall.

RULERSHIP: A planet in its ruling sign is in its rulership, otherwise known as its "domicile," or home position. This is the most authentic and comfortable position for the planet; its energy is strong and raw. Domicile is typically perceived as a beneficial placement, but the uninhibited flow of a planet's energy can bring out both positive and negative qualities.

EXALTATION: A planet located in a sign similar in nature to the sign it rules is in exaltation. Exalted planets can achieve their highest expression, as their energies are softened, beautified, and welcomed. Beyond rulership, this position showcases the planet's best qualities and typically yields favorable results.

DETRIMENT: A planet located in the sign opposite its rulership is in detriment. Planets in detriment feel uncomfortable or stuck, their expression restricted. Adjustments may be needed to unblock the planet's energy.

FALL: A planet in the sign opposite its exaltation is in its fall. Planets in fall seem "out of place" or awkward, their expression weakened. They can express themselves positively, but effort is required to fully realize their energies.

PEREGRINE: A planet in none of the four previous states is considered peregrine, or neutral; its energies are neither strengthened nor weakened.

CRYSTAL BASICS

While astrology's benefits are geared toward insights and internal guidance, the value of crystals extends into the material world. Because they embody a physical form, crystals provide us with the practical means to bring our thoughts to fruition by creating a powerful link between intentions and action.

Intention Setting with Crystals

Intentions help us define our direction and purpose in the present moment. Unlike goals, which concentrate on future outcomes, intentions focus on who we are in the here and now. When we set an intention, we take the first step toward creating the reality we desire by choosing to align with a particular aim, energy, or mind-set. Though intention setting is a powerful act in itself, we must maintain an active connection and commitment to our intentions for them to be fully realized. For example, we may have the intention to meditate more, but unless we prioritize our practice our intention will likely fall behind the many other items on our to-do list. However, if we set a reminder every morning to meditate we have a much better chance of turning it into a daily habit.

Consciously bringing an intention to the forefront of our mind is key to facilitating its progress, yet we often become disconnected from our intentions without realizing it, as external distractions frequently pull our attention away from the present. It can be easy to get stuck in past cycles and old habits or to overly concern ourselves with future plans and decisions. However, when we assign a particular intention or energy to a crystal, simply holding the crystal or seeing it in our physical space can gently redirect our awareness to our original purpose. The grounding and clarity we receive from working with crystals give us the ability to shift the way we currently think and prompt us to begin making the small, positive changes in our lives that lead to a better sense of balance and fulfillment.

Crystal Selection and Care

Whether you're drawn to a crystal's appearance or are looking for one with a specific purpose, trust your intuition when selecting a crystal to work with. This means letting your inner voice guide you toward a stone that feels right and leaning into your choices. In this way, crystal selection is a lot like trying on clothes—when you find a piece that fits you perfectly, you don't second-guess yourself, you just know. To get the most out of your crystals, care for them properly and follow basic safety instructions.

SAFETY: Familiarize yourself with your crystals and their properties before use. Be especially careful when using crystals in or around water, such as in gem elixirs or bath rituals, as some are water soluble and may contain heavy metals or other compounds that can break down when exposed to water or be dangerous when ingested. The specific crystal rituals recommended in this book are deemed safe; if you are designing your own rituals, research appropriate uses for the crystal you select.

STORAGE: Direct exposure to sunlight can fade photosensitive crystals (typically light or transparent ones). When in doubt, keep crystals out of sunlight. Store rough stones separately to prevent them from chipping. During transit, carry your stones in velvet pouches or padded boxes to avoid scratches.

CLEANSING: Crystals absorb and hold energy over time, so you must cleanse them periodically. Doing this is as simple as setting them in a place where the light of a new moon will shine on them overnight, smudging them with sage or palo santo (make sure to purchase these plants from sustainable sources, as they are increasingly overharvested) and then gently wiping them clean, or placing them on top of clear quartz or selenite for twenty-four hours or up to one week for a deep clean. The ideal timetable for cleansing your crystals depends on frequency and intensity of use, but once a month works as general rule of thumb.

CHARGING (OPTIONAL): After you've cleansed your crystals, you can choose to charge them with your intentions by focusing clearly on your intentions as you hold the stones (also known as "programming") or infuse them with special energy to boost their power; setting them under the light of the full moon is one popular charging method.

Chakras

The word "chakra" is interpreted in various ways, but it generally describes the embodiment of a person's energies. The seven main chakras correspond to different areas within the body, starting at the base of the spine and running up to the crown of the head. These focal points are believed to represent and regulate our vital sources of energy and power, from our sense of security to our ability to access our creativity. When a chakra becomes blocked, we may feel an imbalance in one or more areas of our lives. Crystals can be used to open and realign the chakras, as certain stones correspond to various chakras and can be placed on these points to facilitate a harmonious flow of energy. Becoming aware of the correlation between chakras and crystals can complement your meditation practice and serve as a guiding basis for crystal healing.

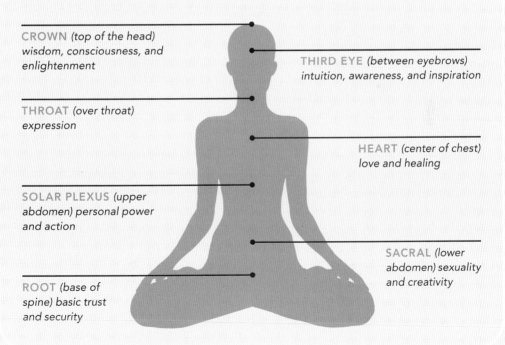

CROWN *(top of the head) wisdom, consciousness, and enlightenment*

THIRD EYE *(between eyebrows) intuition, awareness, and inspiration*

THROAT *(over throat) expression*

HEART *(center of chest) love and healing*

SOLAR PLEXUS *(upper abdomen) personal power and action*

SACRAL *(lower abdomen) sexuality and creativity*

ROOT *(base of spine) basic trust and security*

YOUR CRYSTAL ZODIAC

We all want to embrace mindfulness, but figuring out how to incorporate it into a daily routine can feel vague and overwhelming. Even when the motivation is there, our intentions can get lost or derailed when we try to find the best time, place, and way to be mindful. Your Crystal Zodiac puts an end to cycles of second-guessing by offering a guide to wellness practices and crystal healing based upon your personal astrology, providing clear direction and valuable insights so you can take action now. While discovering the wellness practices that resonate most with you is a beautiful journey, it can take time and a lot of fine-tuning. Your Crystal Zodiac helps you find your footing with greater ease so you can make positive changes today.

The astrological placements in your natal chart, or those of your loved ones, offer tremendous insight into the layers of personality, highlighting strengths and challenges as well as talents and potentials that accompany these layers. By raising awareness of the different areas of life—and of the ways that you, and others, tend to approach them—you can better understand and navigate your own behaviors and relationships, and align with opportunities for growth in your day-to-day.

To begin accessing the wellness benefits of astrology and crystals, look up your major planetary placements to learn their deeper meaning, and discover which crystals best complement their energy using our crystal pairings and mini rituals. Noticing how your Big Three (sun, moon, and ascendant) combine can help you begin to understand the fundamentals of your unique astrological profile, while the personal planets can provide further clarity on specific aspects of your identity. If you know the charts of your friends, family members, or romantic interests, reading their placements can offer a broader perspective of your interactions and provide clues to compatibility. A general sign-inspired ritual and love ritual appear at the end of every zodiac chapter, encouraging you to harness each sign's unique energy and spread the light they share. These rituals can be used by anyone looking to call upon the spirit of a specific sign for guidance and support, and are not exclusive to your sun sign or planetary placements.

Whether you are seeking to jump-start your wellness journey or deepen your existing practice, using astrology and crystals together can not only offer objective insights into your personality but also provide clear, practical applications on how to use them to your benefit.

Discover the cosmic magic that resides in your soul and let your inner spark shine through the guiding observations and empowering rituals that follow in Your Crystal Zodiac.

ARIES

March 21–April 19

Symbol
THE RAM

Quality
CARDINAL

Element
FIRE

Ruling Planet
MARS

Citrine

The first sign of the zodiac, Aries marks the start of another astrological cycle and represents the fire of new beginnings, aligning with the onset of spring, when the dormant seeds of winter suddenly surge with new life. This sign's powerful sense of awakening is connected to themes of identity and self-discovery, as the pioneering spirit of the Ram learns best through firsthand experience.

Like keys in the ignition, Aries's electric spark is ready to take us anywhere if we're willing to climb into the driver's seat and turn the switch. By inspiring us to set aside our fears and fixation on a destination, Aries energy allows us to join in on the joyride of life by taking a leap of faith into the adventure that awaits. Even when the road ahead is difficult or uncertain, Aries energy reassures us that we're exactly where we're meant to be.

When we channel Aries energy, we are able to become our own catalyst for change by accepting the role of self-reliance in carving our own path. William Ernest Henley articulates this sentiment in his poem "Invictus," in the stirring lines, "I am the master of my fate: I am the captain of my soul," which expresses this sign's innate ability to lead and define its future. Ultimately, like the universe, the spirit of Aries is in a state of constant expansion that teaches us that self-confidence and self-belief can provide all the fuel we need to propel ourselves forward and reach for the stars.

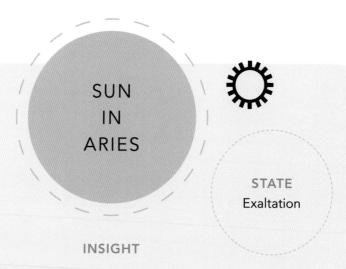

SUN IN ARIES

STATE
Exaltation

INSIGHT

Follow your instincts but don't rush—you're most likely further along than you think.

Like a flash of lightning that ignites the sky, your electric touch breathes life into everything you do. Since the sun rules self-perception, and Aries is known as the sign of the self, your sense of identity and self-confidence are highly developed, as is your need for independence. Daring and fearless, you won't think twice about plunging into the unknown as long as it promises a new adventure. While your fiery will and action-oriented nature make you a dynamic leader, these traits can also cause you to move too quickly. You can afford to slow down and consider all the options to see where your time and energy are best spent long term.

CITRINE

USE FOR: STRENGTH, WILLPOWER, CONFIDENCE, REVITALIZATION

COLOR
Pale yellow to orange brown

CHAKRA
Solar plexus

MANTRA

I can accomplish anything when I connect to my inner fire.

Known as the stone of success, citrine carries the warmth and vitality of the sun and mirrors your radiance and drive to shine. Citrine is the perfect sidekick for sparking your ideas into reality: its motivating energy helps to execute plans and bestows them with staying power.

RITUAL: Attract abundance and good fortune by placing citrine in your workspace, purse, or wallet. Whenever you see the citrine, focus on the prosperity and brightness within you. When you feel rich and fulfilled on an internal level, that mind-set inevitably shines outward, and citrine simply reminds you that you have everything you need to succeed. To combat insecurity, feelings of scarcity, or stagnant energy, hold citrine to the center of your torso, above your navel, and repeat the mantra "I am enough. I have enough. I do enough." Such affirmations keep your positivity and confidence riding high. Abundance breeds abundance.

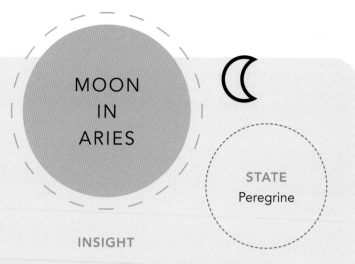

MOON
IN
ARIES

STATE
Peregrine

INSIGHT

Combining logic with emotion leads you to make better decisions and stay focused on your ultimate goal.

Passionate and responsive, you often experience intense feelings and reactive emotions. If you are provoked, your sunny disposition can swiftly dissolve due to your tempestuous nature, causing you to act before you think. While unexpected outbursts or fits of anger are usually short-lived, they can be difficult for the more sensitive or stability-seeking people in your life to stomach. Learning to channel your impulses in a positive way benefits you and your loved ones—physical activities or sports can provide the perfect outlet to blow off excess steam.

LEPIDOLITE

USE FOR: EMOTIONAL BALANCE, STRESS RELIEF, COMPOSURE

COLOR
Lilac, rose violet

CHAKRA
Throat, heart, third eye, crown

MANTRA
*I am able to summon
serenity in any situation.*

Known as the ultimate mood stabilizer and natural tranquilizer of the crystal kingdom, lepidolite is a powerfully pacifying stone and stress-relief aid, useful in quelling anxiety, worry, anger, and fear. The transitional abilities of lepidolite also help to de-escalate any supercharged emotional responses so you can fully process them before making a decision. Whether your feelings range from rage to relaxation, chaos to calmness, lepidolite brings you back to center.

RITUAL: Release tension by unwinding with lepidolite. At least twenty minutes before bed, find a distraction-free place in your home. Sit on the floor and hold lepidolite in your hand for one minute, focusing only on your breath. Afterward, set the crystal aside and begin to gently stretch your body for five minutes, choosing whatever stretches feel best to you. By slowing down and being patient with your physical movements, you encourage your mind to reach a quieter state and let go of the stress of the day. When you are finished, set your lepidolite near your bed for a peaceful, deep sleep, as this crystal is known to alleviate nightmares, insomnia, and restless thoughts.

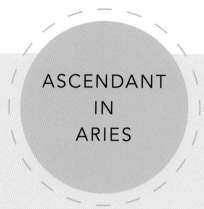

ASCENDANT IN ARIES

*Let your speech inspire change;
your words are powerful.*

Bold and dynamic, you make a first impression that is hard to forget. You possess an entrepreneurial spirit and come across as an energetic self-starter in pursuit of big dreams. Because of your take-charge attitude and larger-than-life persona, you are able to easily captivate an audience and dazzle them with your words, making you an exceptional public speaker. When fired up, you can even make old wallpaper seem exciting—you are a motivating influence in your work or social circles as you rally others to your cause. Be wary of how hot you crank up the heat, however, as your assertive and competitive side can become domineering or bossy at times.

RED JASPER

USE FOR: SHAKING OFF STAGNATION, CENTERING, VIGOR

COLOR
Red

CHAKRA
Root

MANTRA

*I am balanced and in control
of my actions and words.*

Grounding, balancing, and revitalizing, red jasper is an excellent stone for those in leadership positions, providing stability and emotional support in the workplace. This stone prompts you to operate with the highest integrity and brings out your best approaches to new obstacles and conflicts. By regulating your foundational energy, you're able to lead others with a steadier hand.

RITUAL: Gain a fresh perspective toward problem solving and thwart sluggishness by dancing with red jasper. If you're stuck on taking action or are encountering mental blocks, the best remedy is to shake it off! Try fitting an impromptu mini dance break into your day to swing you out of inactivity and boost your mood. You may feel silly at first, but dancing is a quick way to ease any tension that has accumulated in your physical body. Choose a song that matches the red-hot color of this stone to get your blood pumping. Before you begin, hold the stone to the base of your spine and say, "I burn through all blockages," then put it in your pocket or place it nearby and dance for the entire song. By the end, you'll feel completely rejuvenated and able to tackle tasks with a clear mind.

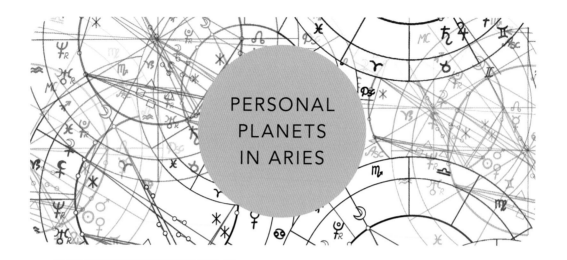

PERSONAL PLANETS IN ARIES

VENUS IN ARIES

STATE
Detriment

INSIGHT

Tug-of-war is more fun when you've met your match.

Your approach to love is like dynamite—fiery, thrilling, and ready to explode. The initial rush of new romance can have you head over heels after a first date, as you live for the thrill of the chase. Because a degree of challenge or conflict stimulates you, your attention can quickly fizzle if boredom sets in. You may find solo pursuits come easier to you than long-term commitments, as passion can be difficult to sustain. Before launching into something new, use the balancing energy of rhodonite to assess what you truly value in a romantic partner and whether there's more to the connection than the lure of fireworks.

MERCURY IN ARIES

INSIGHT

There's a time for bluntness,
but there's also a time for finesse.

You cut to the chase when it comes to communication and don't waste time beating around the bush. Direct and unapologetic, your words erupt like rapid fire. People appreciate your ability to be straightforward, but your opinions can feel rough around the edges at times. Meditating with aquamarine, a stone of calm communication, can help soften your delivery during delicate conversations.

STATE
Peregrine

MARS IN ARIES

INSIGHT

Building with a team, rather than going it alone,
will advance your project further and faster.

Mars is the planet of action, and Aries is all about doing, so you're adept at the start-up. While you can trigger enough momentum to get plans off the ground, finishing is not necessarily your forte, as you prefer handling big-picture decisions more than the fine details. Keeping white howlite, a soothing stone of self-awareness, at your workplace can give you a more patient approach to completing your goals.

STATE
Domicile

ARIES-INSPIRED RITUAL
LEAP OF FAITH

When the future seems uncertain or challenging, channeling Aries energy can feel like grabbing hold of a lifeline. By connecting to the fiery strength of this sign, we learn to become our own hero, protector, and catalyst for change, even in a crisis. If self-doubt or worry are blocking you from taking action, use citrine, red jasper, or any stone that energizes you to feel empowered and confident in your abilities. Meditate with your crystal and allow vitality and warmth to course through your body, then write down three emotions you feel may be limiting you. Afterward, write a positive "I am" mantra for each emotion that helps you counterbalance that feeling. For instance, if you wrote "anxiety," your mantra could be, "I am at ease with each breath I take." Aries symbolizes a point in the zodiac where the past is left behind so a new cycle can emerge, and turning negative emotions into sources of strength is a powerful step in learning to move forward and trusting your capabilities.

PRACTICE SELF-LOVE

Love begins within us, and as the sign of the self, Aries teaches us the importance of prioritizing self-love, as well as the satisfaction of becoming our own lover. If you've been feeling lost—either on your own or in a relationship—or are in need of a spark in your love life, channeling Aries energy can restore your sense of passion, adventure, and independence. Aries understands that although relationships can be a beautiful source of love and support, they aren't what defines us. Each of us has individual needs and desires, and we don't have to rely on others to deliver what we want. Call upon Aries love energy by using rhodonite, green aventurine, or any crystal with compassionate energy to reflect on how you can bring excitement and pleasure to your life. Place your crystal over your heart and listen to what it wants without any judgment. When was the last time you tried a new activity or experience on your own? When was the last time you did something just for you, for no reason other than to treat yourself? After meditating, pick a day on your calendar to take yourself out on a romantic date. Courting yourself can not only be liberating and fun, it can also strengthen the intimate connection you have with yourself by defining your wants and needs, independent from anyone else's. If you're going to invest in someone, why not make it yourself?

TAURUS

April 20–May 20

Symbol
THE BULL

Quality
FIXED

Element
EARTH

Ruling Planet
VENUS

Blue Kyanite

Symbolized by the Bull, Taurus is a sensual earth sign that represents stability and security in the material world, along with enjoyment of life's comforts and pleasures. While Aries offers the seed of a new beginning, Taurus establishes the root system necessary for it to flourish in the physical world. Like the farmer who dutifully sows the field in preparation for harvest time, so the Bull prudently plans for its future and is careful to invest only in endeavors that will yield a fruitful return. This fertile, steady energy works toward building value over time, and understands that, with a solid foundation, the proper resources, and continued effort, a tiny bud can blossom into a full garden, one that nourishes our bodies with food and brings beauty to our spaces for years to come.

When we channel the energy of Taurus, we devote ourselves to creating a garden where we can not only survive but also fully thrive, and we accept the hard work and perseverance needed to make it a reality. Through the eyes of the steadfast Bull, we begin to see fulfillment as a long-term project and view success as a series of steps that we must show up for on a daily basis.

When we feel unmotivated, the enduring spirit of Taurus connects us to our purpose and reminds us that our path is worth pursuing. By allowing Taurus energy to more firmly ground our lives through structure and routine, we are able to find a steady stride and practical rhythm that guide us toward our biggest aspirations. In an ever-changing world, Taurus represents finding a constant we can depend on, a mountain of strength that can help us stand against any storm.

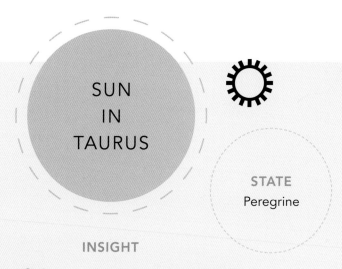

SUN
IN
TAURUS

STATE
Peregrine

INSIGHT

Confidence prepares you to climb a mountain; self-doubt keeps you looking down.

Firmly rooted in the physical world, you bask in the quality and comfort of your surroundings and will go to great lengths to ensure your security. Because you derive pleasure from the senses, the good life for you is one of simple luxuries, such as delicious meals, cozy slippers, and a warm bed. Your ability to savor the moment gives you a relaxing, grounded energy that others like to be around, and your practical outlook allows you to achieve great material success. Because of your self-reliant and responsible nature, you tend to take on a heavy workload—developing robust confidence in your abilities will help you move forward even when you are under stress.

JADE

USE FOR: SELF-AWARENESS, WISDOM, CLARITY, GOOD FORTUNE

COLOR
Vivid green

CHAKRA
Heart

MANTRA

I find peace by discovering my true potential.

The tranquil and protective energies of jade seek harmony above all, making it your go-to stone for achieving peace of mind. Considered by many to be lucky, jade has stabilizing properties that make it the perfect companion for easing you into a state of relaxation, as it gently sloughs away self-doubt and negativity.

RITUAL: Start your day from a place of serenity by using jade in a morning meditation. Upon waking, meditate with jade in your hand for five minutes as you focus on the quality of your breath, remaining present with every slow inhale and exhale. Learning to hold this space for yourself before rushing to check texts or work e-mails can mitigate subconscious stress and infuse your mornings with a tranquility that lasts the entire day.

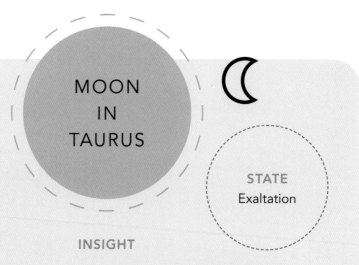

MOON IN TAURUS

INSIGHT

Do not linger in comfort so long that indulgences become necessities.

This fortunate placement paints your emotions with a gentle serenity, as the headstrong aspects of the Bull melt into a soft sweetness when paired with the sensitive moon. Your thoughts and feelings are planted on solid ground, and as long as life feels comfortable and secure there's little that can uproot your calm and steady mood. Your luxurious tastes lead you to seek the finer things in life, but you are rarely ostentatious, and you generously share with those you trust. Much of your time is spent reveling in sensual delights, as you enjoy cooking up a scrumptious meal or sinking into an afternoon siesta. A creature of habit, you may get too used to the comforts you provide yourself, but keeping your motivation in check and your mind open can protect against laziness or inactivity.

SELENITE

USE FOR: CLARITY, CLEANSING, CHANGE, PROTECTION

COLOR
White or transparent

CHAKRA
Crown, third eye

*I am filled with light
and it sets me free.*

Cleansing and purifying, selenite quickly absorbs and unblocks stagnant or dormant energy built up over time, making it an effective stone to facilitate personal growth. In promoting mental clarity, selenite draws you back to the present by improving focus and memory.

RITUAL: Clear away mental fog or sluggishness at work by placing selenite in your office or on your desk. Simply gazing at this elegant, peaceful stone can encourage an energetic reset, as any imbalances that cause you to feel heavy or stuck are instantly washed away. Selenite can also serve as a reminder to move your body—if you can, take a short stretch break to release pent-up physical tension.

ASCENDANT IN TAURUS

INSIGHT

The river of change can lead you to fertile ground.

You possess a silent strength that may initially come off as shyness or standoffishness, yet there is an earthy endurance to you that others find comforting. Whether you are offering practical solutions during a crisis, working late on a project, or providing a steady shoulder to cry on, others know they can count on you to be there. As a result, you are often seen as an anchoring force for those around you, bringing a measured and capable hand to every effort. For this reason, you may excel in managerial roles in finance or other jobs dealing with wealth. While sticking to tried-and-true methods can make life more predictable, you could miss out on valuable opportunities if you remain overly rigid or complacent.

CHRYSOCOLLA

USE FOR: WISDOM, EMPOWERMENT, RELEASE

COLOR
Turquoise, blue green

CHAKRA
Throat, heart

MANTRA

I flow like water over any terrain.

Gentle yet powerful, the reassuring energy of chrysocolla invokes inner strength and balance during times of change. This stone guides you through challenges with serenity and acceptance of all situations, allowing you to trust your intuition and deviate from the comfort of the familiar.

RITUAL: Embrace change by choosing one day a week to openly explore the world with chrysocolla for at least one hour. Before you step outside your house, feel the tranquil energy of this stone dissolve any thoughts of what will happen and keep it in your pocket as you let your intuition guide you. By setting aside time to approach new experiences on a small scale, you begin to associate uncertainty with more positive, rewarding feelings and move beyond your comfort zone on a regular basis.

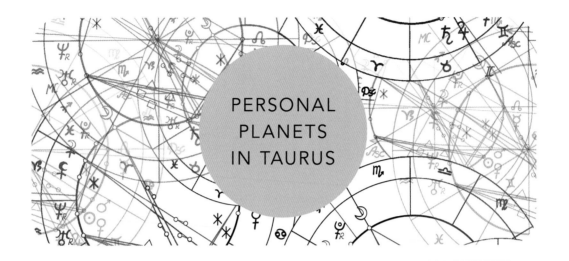

PERSONAL
PLANETS
IN TAURUS

VENUS IN TAURUS

INSIGHT
Abundance is simply a state of mind.

STATE
Domicile

Slow and steady wins the race to your heart. You approach love with a practical eye and take partnership seriously because when you choose to put down roots, you're in it for the long haul. Heavy investment in your relationships makes you an extremely devoted and attentive partner; however, viewing your connections as assets can lead to possessive tendencies, jealousy, or difficulty letting go. Meditating with malachite, a powerful stone of transformation, can help you recognize the difference between spiritual abundance and monetary wealth, and allows you to release your heart from material attachments.

MERCURY IN TAURUS

INSIGHT

Protect your perspective, but don't fortify it to the point that your mind is closed to new ideas.

STATE
Peregrine

Your communication style is genuine, matter-of-fact, and thoughtful. You need time to process all the potential outcomes of a situation before making a decision, and aren't likely to budge once you've made up your mind. Keeping blue kyanite, a stone of communication, near you during negotiations or group projects can help you unite disparate energies and boost your ability to think on the fly.

MARS IN TAURUS

INSIGHT

There's a difference between being patient and being passive.

STATE
Detriment

You are patient and methodical in your actions, resist change, and prefer vigilant planning over improvisation. While your determination to stay the course and persevere until the job is done gives you immense staying power, it can hinder your ability to adapt to new conditions, making you stubborn or immovable. Wearing or carrying bloodstone, a stone of courage and vitality, can offer support during periods of adjustment by stimulating a smooth flow of energy that helps you embrace the situation at hand.

TAURUS-INSPIRED RITUAL
SWEET STABILITY

The tenacious Bull perseveres despite all odds, knowing that success can be attained with a steady pace and committed effort. By tapping into the grounded energy of Taurus, we learn the practical means by which daily progress can be made and find a stable rhythm in our lives. Establishing a skin-care ritual during your morning or evening routine is perfect for connecting to Taurus energy, as this sign enjoys seeing the tangible, physical results of a repeated action. Keeping jade, malachite, or any harmonizing stone in your bathroom can serve as a daily reminder of the action you are taking, whether it's washing your face, applying a serum, or simply brushing your teeth. When you are finished, repeat the mantra, "I am consistent with what I care for." Affirming the tasks we continue to show up for brings a small sense of accomplishment to the day—and it highlights the comfort and stability we can gain from structure.

TURN ON THE SLOW CHARM

Ruled by the decadent and beauty-loving Venus, Taurus calls us to delight in our earthly senses by teaching us how to slow down and savor the moments that bring us pleasure. Cooking is a wonderful way to stimulate and engage all five senses, and, like the patient Bull, it is best when it's not rushed. Relish the process of cooking from start to finish by using chrysocolla or selenite to guide your intuition as you select your ingredients; while your food simmers, hold rose quartz or any love stone as you slowly sink into the sensuality of your space, noticing every smell, sound, and sensation that awakens your body. Before you eat, marvel at what you've created and appreciate the nourishment you're about to receive. Afterward, reflect on how the quality of your experience changed by slowing down and appreciating the present. Life is a string composed of many small moments, and Taurus shows us how to find beauty and pleasure in every one.

GEMINI

May 21–June 20

Symbol
THE TWINS

Quality
MUTABLE

Element
AIR

Ruling Planet
MERCURY

Blue Lace Agate

Whoever said you only live once obviously never met a Gemini. Depicted as the celestial Twins, this inquisitive air sign is characterized by a spritely duality that encompasses a diversity of perspectives, interests, and personas. This fluid energy can shift between opposing views, adapt to any circumstance, and develop new skills with ease, making Gemini the ultimate master of disguise and symbol of reinvention.

The source of Gemini's multifaceted nature stems from the immense reservoir of experience it has to draw from. Ruled by Mercury, the planet of communication, this sign learns through interaction—exchanging ideas and opinions with those around it—and absorbs an impressive amount of information in the process. Always up for an intellectual challenge or verbal sparring match, Gemini needs a continuous stream of mental stimulation in order to keep it engaged. As a result, Gemini energy tends to flit from one subject to another, skimming the surface before moving on to wherever its curiosity takes it. Though it may not stay in one place for very long, the Twins' energy covers twice the ground when it comes to exploring new endeavors.

When we channel the energy of Gemini, we become fascinated by the world and approach life more freely. With this energy, we are not only able to embrace change but openly welcome it into our lives. To variety-loving Gemini, each experience, place, and person offers a special lesson, and its energy calls us to find out what that is. Whether it's a key to unlocking a part of ourselves or another brush for our creative toolbox, Gemini sees every facet of life as a treasure trove of potential, where the number of characters we can become is limited only by the scope of our imagination.

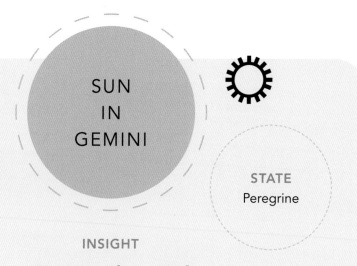

SUN IN GEMINI

INSIGHT

Resting the mind rejuvenates the body.

For the shape-shifting Twins, variety is the spice of life, and you're here to experience all that life has to offer. You approach the world with enthusiasm and wonder, and follow your curiosity to the subjects, people, and places that stimulate your mind. As a result, tying your core identity to anything specific can be difficult—and, frankly, you enjoy this fluidity. You soak up information like a sponge, which makes you adept at conversing on a number of topics, and nothing thrills you more than playing devil's advocate. While your highly active mind makes you a critical thinker, taking a break from all the processing and pondering can prove beneficial in reducing stress.

BLUE LACE AGATE

USE FOR: DIGITAL DETOX, REST, MENTAL EXHAUSTION, BALANCE

COLOR
Light blue with subtle banding

CHAKRA
Throat

MANTRA
I root myself with each breath I take.

The soothing energy of blue lace agate provides a much-needed reprieve to an overstimulated mind. This stone's freeing energy effectively calms nerves and anxiety by quieting the distractions of the external world. When your thoughts are overwhelming, the grounding effects of blue lace agate can give you the space you need to breathe and just be.

RITUAL: Unwind with blue lace agate during the evening by establishing a cut-off time for phone use, preferably an hour or two before bed. Set an alarm every night that prompts you to put your phone away, and keep blue lace agate next to your device. If you find yourself drawn to your phone, reach for this stone instead, taking a moment to breathe deeply as any thoughts are replaced by feelings of peace.

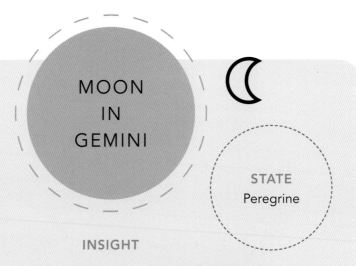

MOON IN GEMINI

STATE
Peregrine

INSIGHT

When you relay the logic behind your feelings, you allow others to keep up with your pace.

Due to your objective, airy nature, your emotions tend to be driven more by thoughts than by feelings. This isn't to say that you don't feel deeply, but you view emotions like pieces of information you can analyze. You also have a propensity for multitasking and compartmentalizing, which makes it nearly impossible for you to linger in a single mood for very long. Others may mistake this emotional agility for flightiness or super-ficiality, but you're simply not interested in mulling over the past. As the moon indicates emotional needs, constant stimulation is what comforts you, so you're always looking toward the future and the new adventures that come your way. When you're bored, your mischievous side can seek stimulation from those around you, so be careful of engaging in gossip, as much as it may satisfy your curiosity.

SERPENTINE

USE FOR: RELIEF FROM EMOTIONAL STRESS AND IRRITABILITY, REGENERATION, HEALING

COLOR
Translucent to opaque shades of green with dark inclusions

CHAKRA
All

MANTRA

I honor my growth by shedding old thoughts and beliefs that no longer serve me.

The regulating and intuitive energies of serpentine bring balance to the emotional body and instill a greater sense of purpose. Curiosity and wandering thoughts are set aside as the wisdom of serpentine encourages you to take responsibility for your feelings and to understand how they affect others. This stone is useful for uncoiling layers of discomfort throughout the body.

RITUAL: Meditate with serpentine to dissolve emotional imbalances caused by restlessness. Hold this stone as you breathe in positivity and exhale negativity, noticing your center growing steadier with each repetition until the cycle feels complete. To help focus your breathing, choose words for what you want to release and attract; for example, release "fear" on the exhale and attract "strength" on the inhale.

ASCENDANT
IN
GEMINI

You have a finite amount of energy, so focus it on the big picture.

Full of charm and wit, you approach the world with an inquisitive eye. Your wide variety of interests leads you to meet people from all walks of life, and as a natural communicator you have no problem breaking the ice. Strangers can become your best friends in a matter of minutes, enchanted by your playful banter and quirky perspective. Eager to learn all you can, you tend to explore multiple interests simultaneously, and sometimes sacrifice depth for extra bandwidth. As a result, you may come across as a "jack of all trades, master of none" type. This isn't to say you aren't capable of mastering a particular craft, though. When you choose to focus your attention, you can develop your skills at an incredible speed. To fully shine, look for a flexible career that requires a diverse skill set and critical thinking to keep you mentally engaged.

BLUE SODALITE

USE FOR: POSITIVITY, COMMUNICATION, SPIRITUAL AWARENESS, AUTHENTICITY

COLOR
Deep royal blue with white veins

CHAKRA
Throat

MANTRA

I support and vocalize my beliefs with clarity.

A stone of wisdom, logic, and inner peace, blue sodalite supports speaking and following your truth. Your duality can pull you in different directions, making it hard to develop a strong sense of self—using this stone can connect you to your greater life path and teach you to trust your decisions.

RITUAL: Place blue sodalite in the northern area of your home or room to facilitate forward momentum in your career or steady progress toward a goal. This placement is associated with the element of water, which supports a positive, balanced flow of energy to carry your intentions. When you encounter a fork in the road and must make an important choice, meditate with blue sodalite for clarity and intuition, visualizing a gentle current of water guiding you ahead.

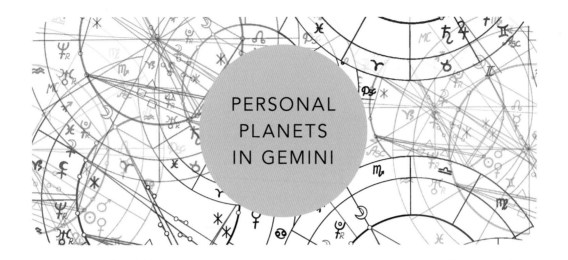

PERSONAL
PLANETS
IN GEMINI

VENUS IN GEMINI

INSIGHT

*Making space for deeper, more intimate
conversations can bring clarity to your connections
and illuminate areas for improvement.*

STATE
Peregrine

You have a flirty, light approach to love and need plenty of room to breathe. Overly regimented or stuffy relationships are not for you. While many suitors attract your eye, the fastest way to your heart—and the surest way to stay there—is through your mind. Because you are a social butterfly, you require a partner who understands your need for freedom; you hold onto love loosely, which may be interpreted as disinterest. Meditating with chrysoprase, a stone of compassion and altruism, can help you make decisions with your heart rather than your head.

MERCURY IN GEMINI

INSIGHT

In a sea of melodies, remember your own unique voice.

STATE
Domicile

You excel at communication and are likely skilled in multiple forms of expression, such as public speaking, podcasts, debates, or teaching. When your mental wheels are rolling, late-night discussions with friends can easily spill into the early morning. You synthesize information quickly but may not always grasp the full concept before forming an opinion. Holding apophyllite, an uplifting and purifying stone, can release you from trivial distractions and prevent you from making snap judgments.

MARS IN GEMINI

INSIGHT

Experience is not always measured by the territory covered.

STATE
Peregrine

You have a fickle, scattered energy that casts a wide net but keeps to the surface. Easily bored, you tend to flutter among activities throughout the day and have a hard time sticking to one project. Your adaptability is well suited to environments that require you to think on your feet, but you may grapple with staying consistent in more structured settings. Keeping blue apatite, a stone of motivation, at your workplace can vastly improve your time management and promote independence.

VERBAL VIRTUOSO

As the mercurial messenger, Gemini is the ultimate communicator of the zodiac, finding expression, freedom, and fascination through words. However, for the rest of us, communication may not happen so easily—we can become so fixated on finding the "right" way to express ourselves that we ignore all other possibilities. In contrast, the energy of Gemini encourages a playful approach to communication by celebrating its various forms, taking note of the unique perspective each provides. Holding blue sodalite or apophyllite can attune you to your inner wisdom and facilitate a positive, unobstructed flow of energy as you explore different modes of expression, such as singing a song, writing a poem, or simply recording a voice memo. Experimenting with multiple media can connect you to messages you may not have been aware of, allow you to examine all the dimensions of your emotions, and, most importantly, help you find your true voice.

MINGLE WITH YOUR MIND

Stimulated by learning and experience, Gemini is a sociable sign that inspires us to find pleasure through the intellectual rapport we establish with others. The communicative Twins ask us to share the interests and passions that excite us, regardless of our experience level, so that we may expand our social circles and opportunities for connection. If you have a hobby you haven't shared with others or want to pursue a new one, call upon Gemini energy to boost your powers of communication and draw fresh connections to you by posting about your interests online. Keeping chrysoprase, blue apatite, or any stone of communication near your phone or computer can promote calm, lighthearted, and authentic self-expression in the details you choose to share about yourself. When you put yourself out there without expectations, you may be surprised by the responses you receive—and these could connect you with others who share your interests. By mingling with other minds and expanding your network, you can open yourself up to a whole world you never knew existed.

CANCER

June 21–July 22

Symbol
THE CRAB

Quality
CARDINAL

Element
WATER

Ruling Planet
MOON

Chalcedony

Soul meets body in the sensitive water sign of Cancer. Symbolized by the Crab and ruled by the motherly moon, this caring sign is guided by the tide of its emotions. There is an intuitive, almost psychic quality to the Crab that represents the intimate connection we have to our feelings and maternal energies, as well as to our sense of home.

Much like a crab lives between water and land, so Cancer moves between the deep sea of intuition and the grounding shore of the physical world. Navigating these environments and their blurring boundaries can be confusing, but as long as Cancer has its protective shell, it can always return to the comfort of home. As the zodiac's ultimate nester, Cancer requires a personal sanctuary—both emotionally and in the physical world—where it can collect its most cherished belongings. Filled with memories and nostalgia, the Crab's "shell" feels familiar and safe, providing a calm refuge in rough waters. During times of stress, Cancer's motherly touch nurtures, comforts, and reassures us.

By connecting to the energy of the tender Crab, we embrace the nourishing waters of our emotions and are filled with a compassionate current that seeks to honor and preserve. Sensitive yet strong, Cancer energy helps us become the keeper of our emotions and the anchor of our shell. This sign teaches us that establishing boundaries is not only a powerful act of self-care, but that the sacred space we hold for ourselves, and our feelings, is what allows us to grow and prosper. When we attune to Cancer energy and the depths of our inner world, we are able to reach the most vulnerable and intimate parts of ourselves, and tap into our intuitive magic.

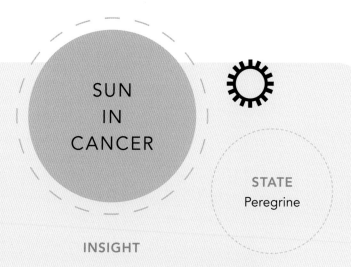

SUN
IN
CANCER

STATE
Peregrine

INSIGHT

You can't pour from an empty cup.

As the moon child of the zodiac, there is a cyclical ebb and flow to your nature that is governed by emotion and intuition. Highly sensitive to your watery world, the slightest change in the environment can affect your mood. You soak up feelings like a psychic sponge and may quickly retreat to the depths of your shell when overwhelmed. Having a safe and cozy space in which you can let your guard down is essential—without an inner sense of security you can feel lost. While your tender heart makes you an excellent nurturer, focusing on your own nourishment is beneficial, as your strong desire to care for others may cause you to lose sight of your own needs.

MOONSTONE

USE FOR: FOCUSED THINKING, CALM, EMOTIONAL BALANCE

COLOR
Colorless with a soft, glowing sheen

CHAKRA
Sacral, third eye, crown

MANTRA
I am aligned with my intuition.

The tender embrace of moonstone balances the emotional body. This gentle, ethereal stone is connected to the moon, your ruling planet, so it is perfect for illuminating your feelings. With its patient and receptive energy, moonstone encourages reflection and growth.

RITUAL: Find your inner anchor by meditating with moonstone on a quiet night. When emotions are uncertain, hold this stone for one minute, then write your thoughts. Afterward, take a relaxing bath or shower and focus on the cleansing water around you. When you are finished, wrap yourself in a cozy blanket and come back to your piece of moonstone, holding it for one minute before again writing your thoughts. Approaching emotions when your physical body is fully relaxed can impact the type of messages you are open to receiving, leading you to deeper insights. Pause to observe the differences in your thoughts before and after you've had a chance to center yourself.

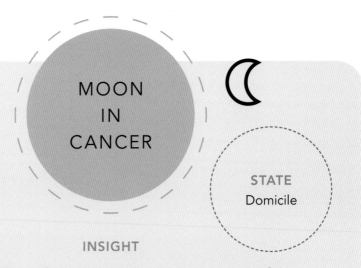

MOON
IN
CANCER

STATE
Domicile

INSIGHT

Don't allow fear to keep you trapped in past cycles. Use your memories to propel yourself forward and make new choices.

The moon is at home in Cancer, meaning that your emotional realm is as deep as the ocean and is more sensitive than that of other signs. Feelings arrive in powerful, unpredictable waves with a forceful pull that can make you feel vulnerable. As a result, you may be defensive or cautious in trusting others, seeking to protect yourself from rejection or hurt. Experiences often leave a lasting impression on you, as you hold onto memories with nostalgia. Your intense emotions feed an abundant imagination and an artist's creative vision; however, these same deep emotions can make it difficult to let go of past wounds.

PINK TOURMALINE

USE FOR: SELF-LOVE, ENCOURAGEMENT, FORGIVENESS, HEALING PAST PAIN

COLOR
Light to hot shades of pink

CHAKRA
Heart

MANTRA

*I am the liberator
of my heart.*

Supportive and healing, pink tourmaline assists in moving you beyond fear to a place of love and compassion. The positive, feminine energy of this stone remedies past blockages that may be holding your heart hostage and can ease you away from emotional extremes. With its soft touch, pink tourmaline melts away feelings of doubt and replaces them with trust.

RITUAL: Release emotional pain or negative attachments that are no longer serving you by meditating with pink tourmaline. When old feelings or harmful thought patterns begin to surface, this stone creates a safe and loving space for you to let go. Rest with pink tourmaline over your heart and repeat the mantra, "I am loved. I am worthy. I am capable." Focus on the sensation of confidence and joy radiating from your heart as the feeling surrounds your whole body.

ASCENDANT IN CANCER

INSIGHT

If you cultivate stability and strength within yourself, you need not seek it in others.

Protected by your hard shell, you initially come off as cool or distant. On the inside you are a big softie, but you tend to be wary of letting new acquaintances have a glimpse into this sensitivity. Letting your guard down requires deep trust and an emotional bond, as you reveal your deepest thoughts only to those in your inner circle. To friends, family, and people you feel "at home" with, you often take on the role of the responsible caregiver, as you wholeheartedly nurture your closest connections. Because of your empathetic nature, you subconsciously absorb the feelings and moods of others, and you may become frustrated and irritable without understanding the reasons. Setting aside plenty of downtime to decompress can help you cultivate control and awareness of your emotional responses.

BLACK KYANITE

USE FOR: CLEARING, HEALING, CONFLICT RESOLUTION

COLOR
Opaque black

CHAKRA
Root

MANTRA

*I release myself from
the ties that bind.*

The grounding and cleansing energy of black kyanite is vital for restoring your emotional reservoirs. This stone provides the ultimate protection against negativity by uprooting unwanted subconscious attachments that may be hindering your growth or healing. If you've listened to a loved one only to feel drained afterward, use black kyanite to purify your energy and stay strong in your power.

RITUAL: Release negative ties by using black kyanite in a cord-cutting ritual. After an emotionally charged or demanding interaction, hold this stone in your hand and locate where in your body you feel stagnant or heavy energy present. Then, visualize cords being drawn from these energetic points. Finally, use black kyanite to trace around your body, cutting through the cords. Taking time to intentionally let go of these ties after a difficult interaction can clear away lingering negative energy.

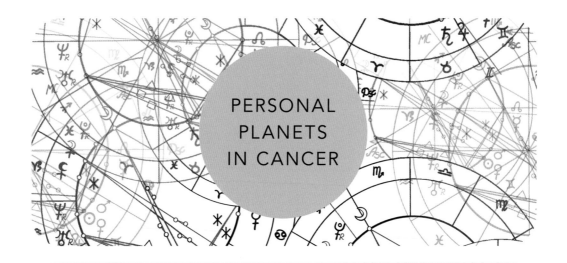

PERSONAL PLANETS IN CANCER

VENUS IN CANCER

STATE
Peregrine

INSIGHT
Real intimacy requires real vulnerability.

Whoever wants to win your heart has to go through your shell, which is easier said than done. You aren't one to jump into a relationship and will take your sweet time when feeling out a potential mate. While you may be cautious at first, once someone has captured your heart, you rarely let go and may dwell in distant memories long after a connection has ended. Meditating with morganite, a gentle stone of love, can help bring forth unexpressed emotions and unresolved pain so you can move forward with an open heart.

MERCURY IN CANCER

INSIGHT

*Sometimes an exchange holds a deeper meaning—
but sometimes words are just words.*

Your thoughts and communication take on an emotional nature, and are subject to your changing moods. You prefer intimate heart-to-hearts over impersonal chitchat, and you may find small talk difficult unless a genuine connection is present. While your sensitivity allows you to pick up on subtle cues beyond the spoken word, it can also cause you to overreact or become defensive when challenged. Wearing chalcedony, a balancing stone, can fine-tune your intuition so that you are receptive to messages without feeling the need to overanalyze them.

MARS IN CANCER

STATE
Fall

INSIGHT

*If you removed fear from the equation,
what would you do?*

Taking action is like crab walking for you, meaning that you tend to approach a situation indirectly. Your desire for a safe outcome makes you adept at strategic planning, and with your intuitive edge, you know just when to make a move; however, your wish for security can also impede your ability to take risks or confront an issue head-on. Holding opal, a stone of self-worth and spontaneity, can provide an instant kick of confidence when you're second-guessing yourself.

CANCER-INSPIRED RITUAL
FENG SHUI FOR THE SOUL

For the security-seeking Crab, there's no place like home. By connecting to the protective energy of Cancer, we honor the spaces closest to us by making them places of positivity and comfort. As Cancer rules the home, placing crystals in different areas of your house or room can attract good energy. Feng shui, in Chinese culture, is a system for arranging surroundings to promote harmony and alignment with the natural world. To attract love or reignite romance, place two pieces of morganite or pink tourmaline next to your bed. For grounding and balance, place moonstone or opal in the center area. For creativity, locate chalcedony in the western area. For protection, place black tourmaline by the front door. When we use feng shui in tandem with crystal energy, we can rest assured that our cozy nest will bring us all the right vibes.

RETURN TO THE WOMB

Finding pleasure in the comfort of home, Cancer calls us to nourish our emotions by returning to a place of familiarity and safety. Taking a love ritual bath featuring rose quartz, morganite, or any stone associated with love can connect us to the waters of our intuition as well as the depths of our heart. As you draw a bath, hold your crystal in your hand as you set your intentions for love, then put it aside. If using rose quartz, you can place it in the tub (be careful of the crystals you add to water, as some are not safe to use this way). Add Epsom salt, lavender essential oil, and rose petals to the bath, then step in. Before submerging yourself, repeat this mantra: "I am cradled by a love that fills my soul." Close your eyes and allow the warm water to embrace you like a cosmic womb, birthing your new intentions.

LEO

July 23–August 22

Symbol
THE LION

Quality
FIXED

Element
FIRE

Ruling Planet
SUN

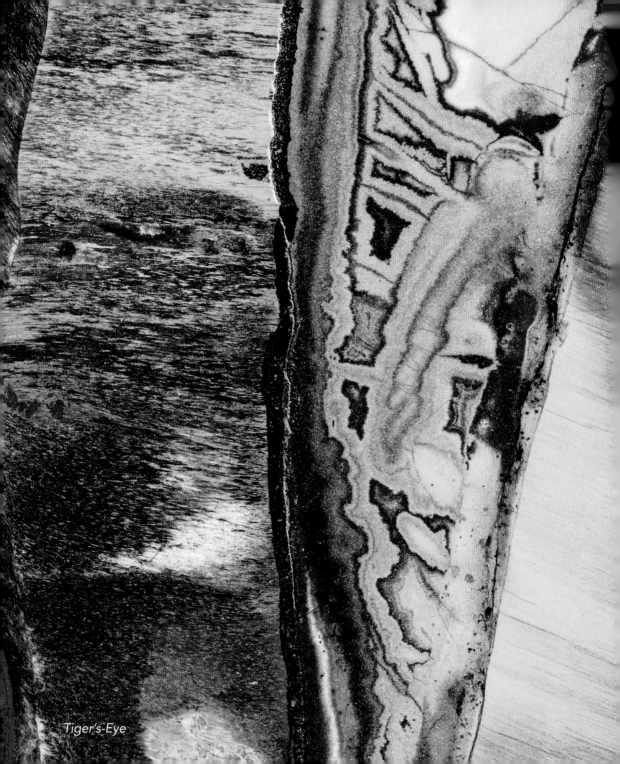

Tiger's-Eye

I f all the world's a stage, no one shines brighter in the spotlight than Leo. Symbolized by the regal Lion, this radiant fire sign represents creative self-expression and benevolence, as well as celebration of the individual. Much like its ruling planet the sun, which sits at the center of our universe, Leo takes center stage as the star of its own story, and its narrative revolves around the path it must travel to step into its unique light.

The tale of the Lion signifies the personal journey we must take in becoming our own person and embracing what sets us apart from the rest of the world. What do we love about ourselves, what makes us special, and how can we express and honor our one-of-a-kind spark? These are the questions the Lion encourages us to answer as we develop a genuine sense of self and discover outlets for authentic expression.

Leo teaches us that when we celebrate ourselves and are filled with confidence, we can connect to the joyous light within our soul and inspire others through our warmth and generosity. However, we cannot accomplish this if we remain behind the scenes, as Leo energy demands that we claim the leading role. No one can tell our story better, and when we claim our own truth we shine our brightest. Ultimately, in connecting to the spirit of the noble Lion, we learn what it truly means to act from the heart and glow with a love so big that even the darkest shadows seem to disappear.

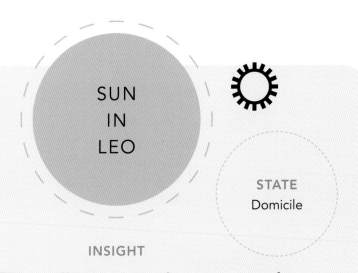

SUN
IN
LEO

STATE
Domicile

Reviewing collective goals as you make decisions can balance out ego-driven influences and lead you to clearer choices.

Lights, camera, action! With your big personality and radiant presence, the world is your runway and you're leading the show. Basking in the full brilliance of the sun, your ruling planet, you shine when you are in front of an audience that can appreciate your unique light. The cheerful glow and optimism you possess can brighten the gloomiest days, making you pleasant to be around. Because self-expression is important to you, you pour your heart into creative endeavors and see your work as a reflection of yourself. However, this strong attachment means that you may be unable to tell when it's time to move on, and you sometimes stick with a task out of a sense of duty or pride. If you can view surrender and admission of fault as a sign of strength instead of weakness, you will be able to handle any setback with wisdom and grace.

TIGER'S-EYE

USE FOR: STRENGTH, CONFIDENCE, WILLPOWER, POSITIVITY

COLOR
Golden brown with red-brown or
dark-brown banding

CHAKRA
Sacral, solar plexus

MANTRA

*I can illuminate the
darkest shadows.*

A stone of authenticity and integrity, tiger's-eye promotes wise use of power and control with its grounding and balancing energy. This stone is essential for understanding your limitations as well as recognizing your strengths and special skills. If you are working with others, tiger's-eye encourages you to delegate responsibilities and maintain an unbiased perspective.

RITUAL: See yourself from a different angle by taking a photo with tiger's-eye. Hold this stone in your hands and rub it for one minute while you allow its pure, warming energy to reveal your true self, visualizing superficial layers of ego or pride dissolving in the process. Then, set up a phone or camera a few feet away and take your photo with a self-timer (do not hold the camera in your hand). Afterward, look at the photo and evaluate the qualities you want to embrace more fully, and the ones you want to release. Viewing yourself from a more remote perspective and in your authentic light can help you assess yourself more clearly, as it allows you to step back from your usual judgments.

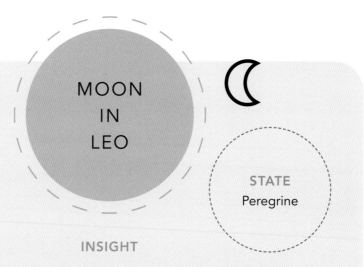

MOON IN LEO

STATE
Peregrine

INSIGHT

Your friend's victories are your victories too, so celebrate them fully.

This placement brings all the sunshine of the friendly Lion to the realm of your emotions, meaning you love big, laugh hard, and always look on the bright side of life. Because the moon is a more private planet, you may not be as comfortable or outgoing in the public eye as a Leo sun, but you do enjoy being the center of attention in the company of family and friends. You shine most brilliantly when you feel admired, confident, and are given lots of love, and will gratefully beam the support and affection you receive back to others. However, if you begin to feel threatened, you may steer more attention toward yourself in an effort to reassert your authority. If you remember that another person's light can never dim your own, you can continue to share with others the generosity you're known for.

LABRADORITE

USE FOR: SPIRITUAL AWARENESS, MENTAL EXPANSION, BREAKING HABITS

COLOR
Dark smoky gray with an iridescent flash

CHAKRA
Third eye

MANTRA

I welcome transformation into my life.

The intuitive and transformational properties of labradorite facilitate powerful internal growth by helping to rise above ego-driven demands and align with a higher level of consciousness. Excellent for introspection, labradorite allows you to take a deeper dive into your emotions while remaining open to shifts in perspective.

RITUAL: Navigate challenges by meditating with labradorite to illuminate the truth. When uncomfortable feelings surface, lie down and place this stone on your forehead, then close your eyes. Focus on your inhale and exhale until you've arrived at a quiet place in your mind, then let your intuition guide you to the insights you seek. By allowing the calm and clearing energy of this stone to bring you to a place of peaceful receptivity, you will be able to communicate with your highest self and dispel any illusions or initial reactions that are blocking you from the greater meaning of your feelings.

ASCENDANT IN LEO

INSIGHT

External validation provides only temporary security and happiness. Find longer-lasting success and fulfillment through increased self-worth.

Dramatic and showy, no one makes an entrance quite like you. Whether you're walking the red carpet or going to work, you present yourself in a grand manner, ready to dazzle and entertain. You come across as a brightly spirited individual with a regal character and often take on the role of the leader with your commanding presence. Feeling admired and respected is important to you, so you go to great lengths to distinguish yourself from others and gain recognition for your achievements. While these factors fuel your ambitions and drive you to work hard, you may view the external validation and approval you receive as an indicator of your self-worth. Embracing your intrinsic value and power will allow you to operate without the need for approval.

SUNSTONE

USE FOR: VITALITY, SELF-ESTEEM BOOST, WORK-LIFE BALANCE, OPTIMISM

COLOR
Peachy, clay-toned coral

CHAKRA
Root, sacral, solar plexus

MANTRA

I am a benevolent beacon of light.

Known as a stone of leadership, sunstone promotes personal power and reflects the openness, warmth, and clarity of light. Working with this stone can help unlock self-imposed limitations, as fears and doubts are replaced by confidence and strength.

RITUAL: Step into your full power and attract new opportunities by using sunstone at work. For increased reach or visibility, place this stone next to your computer or on your office desk to successfully promote your career or advertise your business. Keeping sunstone within sight can also serve as a reminder to follow your higher path when debating a decision, as its joyful glow reveals the noblest course of action. If you feel pulled toward negative habits or destructive tendencies, hold this stone for two minutes and envision the light of the sun sparking within you and radiating outward. Your strength and resolve will be restored.

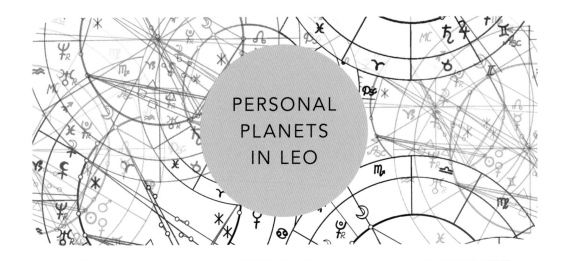

PERSONAL PLANETS IN LEO

VENUS IN LEO

INSIGHT

Showing vulnerability is a sign of strength, not weakness.

The romance-loving Lion rules the heart, which means you're happiest when wrapped up in a sweeping love affair. Generous and dramatic, you tend to express your affection in over-the-top ways and expect the same in return. In a relationship, you need to feel like the first priority and require consistent acts of devotion to keep the sparks flying. While not shy, you're more sensitive than you let on, and may take some time to recover from emotional wounds. Wearing rhodochrosite, a stone of self-love, on a necklace close to your heart can invoke emotional healing and release past pain.

MERCURY IN LEO

INSIGHT
Use your roar on the stage,
not in your personal life.

STATE
Fall

You are expressive in communication and have a knack for storytelling. Conversations are like a performance to you, as your speech has a theatrical flair. You relay your ideas with such confidence that others usually agree, though you rarely back down when your perspective is challenged. Keeping larimar, a stone of calm communication, near your phone or computer ensures that your mind-set remains open and flexible during interactions. Due to larimar's photosensitivity, it is best used in indoor settings away from sunlight.

MARS IN LEO

INSIGHT
Share your evolution, but don't let that
display distract you from your path.

STATE
Peregrine

You are drawn to work and activities that allow you to perform for others and express yourself. Your ability to transform anger, frustration, or negative emotions into artistic endeavors is extremely therapeutic. Though this is a valuable skill, you may start to put these moments of private, internal growth on display for others as a public show. Meditating with carnelian, a grounding and passionate stone, during periods of transformation can shift your focus away from the ego and toward authentic expression, so you can fully honor the creative process.

BRILLIANCE BOOSTER

The benevolent Lion nurtures the light within in order to share it. By tapping into Leo's inner fire, we learn to bask in our own brilliance and inspire others to do the same. During the morning, find a quiet place for self-reflection before you go about your day, and hold tiger's-eye, sunstone, or carnelian in your hand for five minutes as you feel confidence and vitality surge through your body. Then, grab a sticky note and write three positive "I am" statements; affix the note to your bathroom mirror to remind you of the wonderful qualities you possess. For instance, you could write, "I am powerful. I am fearless. I am caring." Afterward, take another note and write three positive "You are" statements about a loved one; give the note to the person at the next opportunity. While self-care isn't always easy to do, not all of its activities involve digging up pain or confronting fears. Sometimes, what we really need is to love and appreciate who we already are. When we are kind and compassionate toward ourselves and others, our inner light can never be dampened.

RECHARGE YOUR HEART

Leo rules the heart, and calls us to heal and charge our own so it can remain strong, open, and full of warmth. When our heart is balanced and open we are able to give and receive love, but when our heart has blockages we can feel disconnected from our emotions and closed off to those around us. A heart meditation exercise with rhodochrosite, rose quartz, or any love-related stone can be helpful in mending old emotional wounds and releasing past trauma. In a dark room, light a single candle and place it on a nonflammable surface as you lie down and close your eyes with your stone over your heart. Focus on your breathing and the feeling of unconditional love and support emanating from the center of your chest, growing with each rise and fall. Take ten deep breaths and envision a faint, pink glow around your heart, which slowly begins to heal as the glow gets brighter. Repeat the breaths until your heart and light feel fully restored. Letting go of past pain can be difficult, especially if you've been holding on to it for a long time, so be gentle and patient with yourself during this exercise.

VIRGO

August 23–September 22

Symbol
THE VIRGIN

Quality
MUTABLE

Element
EARTH

Ruling Planet
MERCURY

Peacock Ore

I n order to see the bigger picture clearly, you have to examine its pieces closely, and no one is better at putting together a puzzle than Virgo. Symbolized by the Virgin or Maiden, this analytical earth sign represents attention to detail, organization, and the quest for perfection. Dedicated to improving all aspects of life, Virgo uses systems and routines to achieve success, and keeps a watchful eye on which methods produce the best results. Perceptiveness is a key Virgo quality, and parsing complex data is one of its greatest skills.

When we channel Virgo energy, we become careful in our observations and are able to bring order to the chaos around us. For this sign, life is like a complicated puzzle to be solved, full of thousands of seemingly unrelated pieces. At first, many of us rush to finish the puzzle without considering what we are trying to form, which makes us likely to overlook critical clues. With Virgo energy, however, we are diligent in studying the details of every piece, no matter how mundane or minute they may seem.

By breaking intricate concepts into their individual components, we are able to better understand their relation to one another, and we learn the proper way to connect them. Through Virgo energy, we understand patterns, identify problems, and form solutions—and our view of the world becomes clearer. This sign shows us that researching the links between the different parts of our lives is an arduous task, but it is worth the effort because, once we grasp how our systems fit together, we can focus on what is truly meaningful to us and work with a greater sense of purpose.

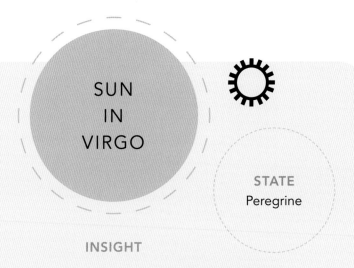

SUN
IN
VIRGO

STATE
Peregrine

INSIGHT

Progress is not always made in giant leaps and bounds—celebrate the small victories along the way.

A place for everything and everything in its place—that is the Virgo code. A lover of order and harmony, you are exceptional at dealing with the details of life, and are drawn to meaningful service. Analytical, intellectual, and helpful, you are interested in reaching your full potential and assisting others so they can do the same. Prestigious awards and fancy titles don't appeal to your modest profile, as rewarding work for you isn't based on salary or recognition but rather on serving a purpose beyond yourself. Your talent for implementing successful methods and maintaining attention to detail makes you a valuable asset to any team, but the pressure to produce perfect work means that you may be critical of yourself and others. Before examining faults with a magnifying glass, remember that constructive criticism is the key to growth.

AMAZONITE

USE FOR: EMPOWERMENT, SUPPORT, COMPASSION, ACCEPTANCE

COLOR
Bright bluish green

CHAKRA
Heart, throat

MANTRA
I am my greatest advocate.

Referred to as a stone of truth and a stone of courage, amazonite bolsters self-awareness, confidence, and the strength to embrace innate abilities without fear or judgment. This stone is essential for releasing perfectionistic tendencies and irrational thoughts that cloud your perspective, and gently calms the mind for balanced, clear thinking.

RITUAL: De-stress after work with a daily meditation using amazonite. Find a quiet place to lie down, place this stone over your heart, and focus on your breath as you quiet your mind, paying attention to any areas of tension or tightness in your body. Focus on one area at a time, and feel the soothing energy of amazonite slowly loosen these points as you take ten deep inhales and exhales. Repeat until all areas are light and relaxed, then say the following mantra: "I cleanse away today's worries and hold space for my own happiness." Practicing this meditation daily can prevent stress and negativity from accumulating and establish a clear break between work and personal time.

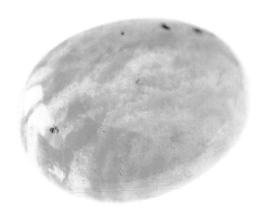

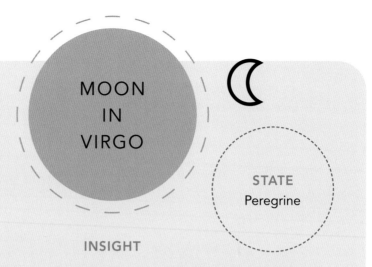

MOON IN VIRGO

STATE
Peregrine

INSIGHT

Failure is a remarkable teacher; don't let fear dissuade you from testing yourself.

For the regimented Virgo, a daily routine isn't just a physical practice, it's an emotional need. You find comfort in purifying and grounding activities that improve your overall well-being, and you are vigilant about incorporating them into your day-to-day life. Crossing another item off your list helps you feel like you're on the right track, and structure allows you to tackle tasks systematically. While your search for perfection makes you an efficient worker, you may get bogged down with nailing every detail and miss the bigger picture or stifle your creativity. There's nothing wrong with holding high standards, but if your expectations become unreachable, you may feel anxious and discouraged. When you begin to believe in your abilities, there's no limit to how high you can soar.

CARNELIAN

USE FOR: MANIFESTATION, OPTIMISM, PASSION, CREATIVITY

COLOR
Red orange to red brown

CHAKRA
Sacral

MANTRA

*I glow in my power and
rise to take action.*

The vivid burst of carnelian's color reflects the richness of its vitality and joy. Through its energizing and balancing properties, this stone casts away pessimism and sluggishness to warm your entire being. In the vibrant rays of carnelian, your outlook brightens as you find the motivation and inspiration to follow your dreams.

RITUAL: Start your day with carnelian for a refreshing energy boost. Upon waking, take carnelian in your hand as you do a simple, easy arm stretch, holding for fifteen to twenty seconds. Pass the stone to your other hand as you switch arms to exercise your other side, and begin to feel a surge of energy and positivity coursing through your body. Then, ask yourself, "What area of my life can I take action in today?" Keep it simple! Performing this brief morning ritual before diving into work can not only ground and energize your physical body, it can also ward off mental lethargy and improve your focus.

ASCENDANT
IN
VIRGO

INSIGHT

Be objective in the way you monitor change. Do not fear what may result, simply prepare for it.

Meticulous and organized, you come off as a type A personality with an impeccable work ethic and professional presence. Responsibilities often fall on your shoulders because you are capable and trustworthy. Careers involving incremental work in a step-by-step approach, such as editing, research, physical therapy, or cooking, help you shine. You place heavy emphasis on health and take exercise and nutrition seriously, sometimes to an obsessive degree. Because you are sensitive, anything that threatens your balance can wreak havoc on your nerves. You may find it difficult to relax until you've taken care of all your duties. No matter how painstaking a task is, you insist on following through and may judge those who fall short or choose to cut corners. Though your diligence is one of your strongest assets, it can come off as self-righteousness at times. Blending emotion with logic can help in softening your matter-of-fact perspective.

SMOKY QUARTZ

USE FOR: FOCUS, STABILITY, SERENITY, POSITIVE THOUGHTS

COLOR
Light grayish brown to deep black

CHAKRA
Root

MANTRA

I am rooted in my actions and intentions.

Banish bad vibes with the powerfully cleansing and anchoring properties of smoky quartz. Protective and detoxifying, this stone eliminates fear, doubt, and worry by absorbing negative energy. When you feel overwhelmed or shaken by obstacles, reach for this stone to bring yourself back to center, and you'll feel your power return.

RITUAL: Purify and protect any space with smoky quartz. For improved cooperation at work, place this stone in your office. To reduce anxiety about traveling, keep smoky quartz in your car or carry it with you on trips. To lessen distractions at home, place this stone near your computer or phone. For a peaceful sleep, set this stone at the foot of your bed to alleviate nightmares and insomnia. Wherever you go, taking smoky quartz with you can create a clear and tranquil environment.

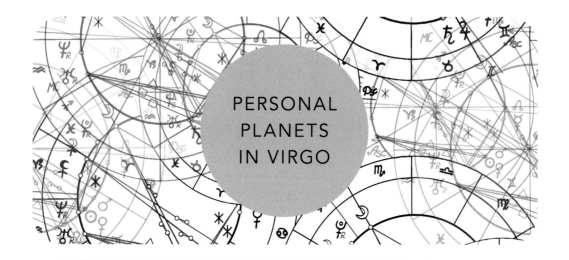

VENUS IN VIRGO

STATE
Fall

INSIGHT

*Expressing frustrations or desires to your partner
through constructive dialogue rather than criticism
allows the messages to be better received.*

You are a staunch realist when it comes to love, and you won't waste time chasing romantic fantasies or getting lost in idealistic pursuits. Not easily swayed by emotion, you need a version of love that has a purpose and makes sense in the real world. When committed, you express your love through your tireless dedication and willingness to work on the relationship, and take pride in being an ample provider. Though you are an extremely supportive lover, you may become fussy or overly critical of your partner, constantly pinpointing areas of improvement. Meditating with peridot, a cleansing stone, over your heart can help to highlight the positives of the present by transforming agitation and resentment into patience and compassion.

MERCURY IN VIRGO

STATE
Domicile

INSIGHT

Fixing others' problems isn't your full-time job.
Don't feel guilty about putting yourself first.

No stone is left unturned with your analytical eye. You are quiet and keen in your observations and have a modest communication style. In organized environments, you have a great capacity for learning and you function best when you're flying with a plan. Because you are adept at problem solving and enjoy assisting others, people often enlist you for help. Wearing moss agate, a stone of intuition and protection, safeguards against overextending yourself by supporting and prioritizing your own growth.

MARS IN VIRGO

STATE
Peregrine

INSIGHT

When you accept that you are exactly where you need
to be, you'll find that joy is available in every moment.

Your desire for productivity causes you to take on many tasks at once, but you're practical, so you can handle heavy workloads effectively. Having too much free time may actually make you restless: your nervous energy needs the healthy channel of frequent activity. You are humble and gentle, and you have a particular way of doing things, especially with regard to work, and will stand by your systems and methods. You want to be good at what you do, so you may be more disheartened by setbacks than others. Keeping peacock ore, an uplifting stone, in your workspace allows you to appreciate the lessons of any situation.

ORDER OF OPERATIONS

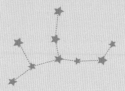

For vigilant Virgo, any problem can be solved with an in-depth analysis and a well-formed plan. Through Virgo energy, we learn how to handle practical matters and daily duties by breaking our work into stages. If you've been putting off a task that feels overwhelming, such as preparing for a move or joining a gym, use smoky quartz or amazonite to calmly form a strategy. Grab a piece of paper and something to write with, then sit at a desk with the stone in your hand. Close your eyes and meditate for two minutes, releasing any negative thoughts or emotions. Afterward, place the stone on your desk and write each step needed to complete your task from start to finish. If you want to join a gym, the steps may be: 1) calculate a budget, 2) research nearby gyms that fit your budget, 3) tour the gyms you like, and 4) finalize your decision and sign up. Making a list that outlines not only what you want to do but also how to do it can help you accomplish your goals more efficiently.

ROOTED IN REALISM

Virgo's sensible nature calls for a practical approach to romance. This sign prompts us to get real about love and pay attention to the nitty-gritty details of our connections, which we often choose to overlook. For a dose of Virgo realism, find a quiet place outdoors to clarify and ground your intentions. Stand or sit with the soles of your feet firmly planted on the ground (for best results, practice barefoot) to access Virgo's earth energy; then, hold peridot or any love-related stone over your chest. Breathe deeply and visualize a white light surrounding your heart for one minute. Afterward, focus on guiding the light down through your feet and deep into the earth in the form of roots. Once you feel stable and centered, ask yourself whether your current relationship or partner aligns with your personal values. Are your needs being met? Have you compromised your ideals or standards? If so, why? Be specific! When firmly planted in Virgo's anchoring energy, we are able to dispel the illusions that prevent us from finding true fulfillment in love.

LIBRA

September 23–October 22

Symbol
THE SCALES

Quality
CARDINAL

Element
AIR

Ruling Planet
VENUS

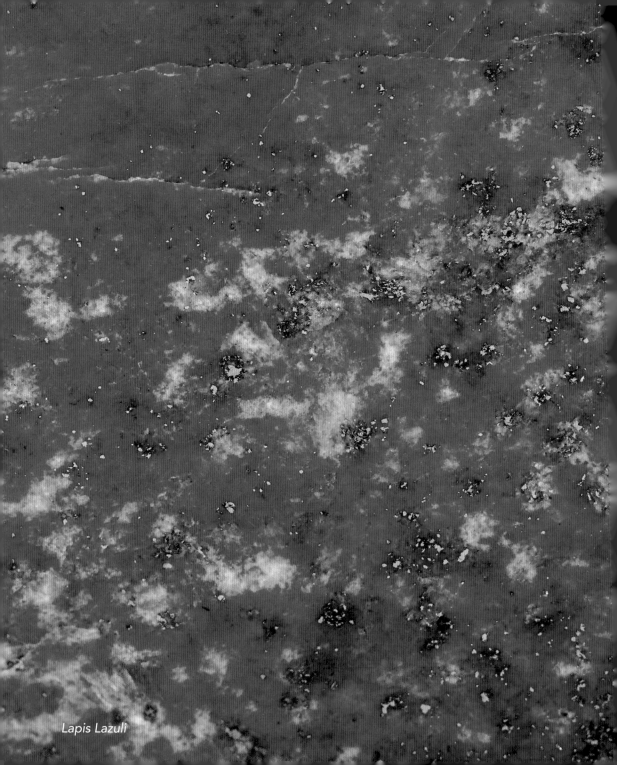
Lapis Lazuli

Libra represents the halfway point in the astrological cycle—the beginning of its season falls on the autumnal equinox, a point in the year when day and night are equal. It's no surprise, then, that Libra is a sign of balance, and is appropriately depicted by the Scales. Concerned with finding symmetry, beauty, and harmony, this sign prefers cooperation over confrontation and uses its charm to keep the peace, especially in partnerships.

When we channel Libra energy, we strive to bring balance to our lives by promoting unity and justice in our relationships. Through this sign, we shift from "I"- to "we"-centered thinking to cultivate a greater sense of togetherness and find equilibrium in our connections. Libra understands that harmony cannot be achieved if arguments and perspectives are one-sided, and it sees a willingness to compromise as a strength rather than a weakness.

By connecting to the diplomatic energy of Libra, we are able to approach problems with an objective eye and seek solutions that are fair to all parties. When discord and division occur, Libra energy builds a bridge to meet others halfway. For this sign, equations are not solved with absolutes: acceptable answers require that we acknowledge all the variables at play and adjust accordingly. The overall insight granted by Libra energy can be summarized by Isaac Newton's third law of motion, commonly stated as: "For every action, there is an equal and opposite reaction." When applied to relationships, this concept helps us recognize that every action we take and each decision we make has an impact on both parties, and this allows us to tip the scales back to center in this delicate balancing act we call life.

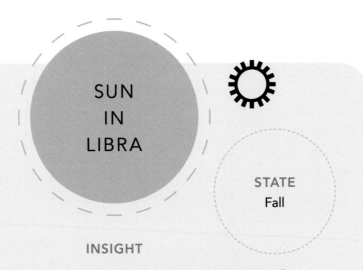

SUN IN LIBRA

STATE
Fall

INSIGHT

Clarifying your goals at the outset of any endeavor can prevent ambivalence from impeding your progress.

It's hard for anyone to resist a Libra. Elegant, graceful, and armed with charm, you are highly perceptive of others' needs and know how to make people feel comfortable. No matter who you're talking to or what you're talking about, your ability to balance a conversation or finesse a negotiation is unmatched. You seek peace and harmony above all, and use your diplomatic grace and understanding of partnerships to facilitate cooperation and settle conflict. Adept at finding the common threads among different groups of people, you are skilled at weaving multiple objectives together in a way that is fair to all. While this makes you an exceptional mediator, your desire for unity and connection can make finding and expressing your individual identity more difficult.

AMETRINE

USE FOR: TRANSFORMATION, ACCEPTANCE, BALANCE, MENTAL CLARITY

COLOR
Purple and golden yellow

CHAKRA
Solar plexus, crown

MANTRA

I am confident and deliberate in my choices, and pursue my goals with ease.

The clarifying properties of amethyst and the strengthening qualities of citrine combine to form this uniquely powerful stone. As soothing as it is stimulating, the dual energies of ametrine work to balance masculine and feminine forces and harmonize thoughts and actions. Equip yourself with this stone to leave confusion behind and move forward in your decisions.

RITUAL: Combat indecisiveness or contradictory thoughts by using ametrine to tip the scales toward the energy you need in any given moment. Flip a coin before meditating with this stone to determine whether to focus on the calming properties of amethyst (heads) or the motivating properties of citrine (tails). If you feel called to both energies, simply use both: first, allow the tranquil energy of amethyst to quiet your mind and guide your direction. Then, follow up by drawing on the empowering energy of citrine to implement the changes you want to make.

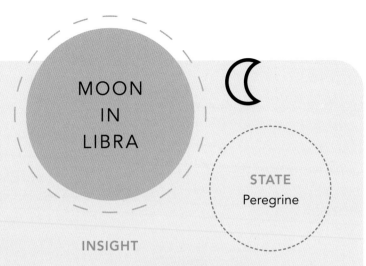

MOON IN LIBRA

STATE
Peregrine

INSIGHT

To honor your true feelings, you must cultivate independence.

Your inner world feels harmonious and safe when your relationships are balanced. Easygoing and relaxed, you respond to the feelings of others by mirroring their moods. If coupled, you bond with your partner by sharing and supporting your loved one's emotions, and find that confrontation and hostility can be avoided through mutual agreement. Because relationships offer you security, you typically do not remain single for long, and are quick to solidify your connections. While your willingness to compromise is useful for navigating partnerships, it can also cause you to remain in toxic cycles or accept circumstances that do not satisfy your needs. The ability to discern which connections truly fulfill you and which offer superficial gratification or comfort holds tremendous long-term value.

WHITE OPAL

USE FOR: SELF-WORTH, SURMOUNTING MENTAL OBSTACLES, AWARENESS, LOYALTY

COLOR
Milky white or cream with flashes of iridescence

CHAKRA
Crown

MANTRA

I awaken to my inner self and act on my pure intentions.

Balancing and strengthening, opal enhances freedom of self-expression by encouraging you to trust your feelings and take responsibility for them. The illuminating properties of this stone reveal past patterns and behaviors, leading you toward change and a deeper sense of self. Though initial work with this stone can feel especially intense, the cleansing you experience is necessary for attuning to your higher purpose.

RITUAL: Transform negative emotions into empowering statements with white opal. Hold this stone in your hand as you feel its purifying, soothing energy softly dissolve inhibitions and fears. If a negative feeling remains, state it out loud and name a positive quality you possess that can help you handle it. For instance, if you are anxious, you could say, "I am feeling anxious, but my patience allows me to remain grounded and calm."

ASCENDANT
IN
LIBRA

INSIGHT

Saying no and establishing boundaries are important parts of your personal and professional development.

Amicable and charming, you make a pleasant first impression and are easy to like. Your gentle and unassuming quality makes you effortless to be around, allowing you to breeze through multiple social circles and attract many friends. You have a diplomatic presence and often take on the role of the peacekeeper or mediator due to your desire for harmony. Careers that involve personal relations or negotiation in some form, such as law or sales, are where your social savvy and graceful persuasion shine. Though your agreeable nature makes you popular, you have a tendency to be a people pleaser and should be mindful of your own needs in relation to others.

AGATE

USE FOR: COURAGE, SECURITY, BALANCE, COMPOSURE

COLOR
Varied; opaque or semitransparent with banding

CHAKRA
All (specific to color)

MANTRA

I am the master of my reality.

The abundance of agates to choose from means this stone is incredibly accessible; no matter the type, its supportive and nurturing properties make it an ideal companion for personal growth. This stone offers a heightened grasp of reality by facilitating honest introspection and self-analysis. In helping you understand and accept who you truly are, agate inspires confidence and strengthens self-respect.

RITUAL: Improve self-awareness and find your direction by meditating with agate. Hold this stone in your hand or rub it between your thumb and forefinger to reach a quiet state. Then, think of an area of your life you have recently improved and take a minute to celebrate this accomplishment. Afterward, consider an area of your life that needs attention and take a minute to contemplate your first step toward your goal. Acknowledging your growth so far and noting where to shift your efforts next lets you check on your own progress and fosters a balanced, grounded outlook.

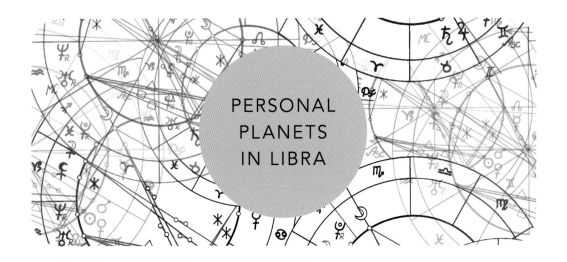

VENUS IN LIBRA

STATE
Domicile

INSIGHT

Look for addition, not completion, in your partnerships.

Bust out the candles and rose petals because love is in the air! This placement marks you as the ultimate romantic in the search for eternal union. You wear your heart on your sleeve and get instantly starry-eyed over the prospect of true love, as partnerships are where you thrive. Others are drawn to your magnetic appeal and style, which makes entering relationships easier for you than most. While this is a wonderful placement, your desire to blend with another can develop into codependency if left unchecked. Placing two pieces of rose quartz, a stone of universal love and compassion, next to your bed can help promote a healthy balance in the way you give and receive love.

MERCURY IN LIBRA

INSIGHT

Be open to others' opinions without dismissing your own.

STATE
Peregrine

Your communication style is tactful, discerning, and delicate. You shy away from situations that force you to make snap judgments, as you prefer to carefully weigh the pros and cons of your decisions. Your commitment to fairness dominates your thoughts, which is why others trust that your opinions are well reasoned. However, if you straddle both sides of an issue too long, people may find your behavior exhausting or confusing. Keeping lapis lazuli, a stone of higher wisdom and learning, on your desk as you write memos or talk with others can bring deeper awareness to your beliefs and facilitate authentic self-expression.

MARS IN LIBRA

INSIGHT

Indecision is like treading water—it can keep you afloat, but it won't help you reach the shore.

STATE
Detriment

You believe there are many ways to achieve a goal, but deciding which one is optimal can present difficulties. In considering all your options and their potential outcomes, you may become fixated on finding the absolute best way to approach a problem rather than taking steps to actually solve it. Though this ability lends itself well to forecasting, theorizing, and adjusting to changing variables, it can make picking a course of action and sticking to it challenging. Wearing or carrying clear quartz, a stone of clarity, on your body can combat ambiguous or conflicted thoughts by improving focus and concentration.

CHECKS AND BALANCES

L ibra's Scales are a symbol of balance, and this sign's energy encourages us to harmonize the various aspects of life to create a well-composed whole. Use clarifying or truth-enhancing stones such as clear quartz, lapis lazuli, or agate to take a monthly inventory of where you are spending the majority of your time and energy; this can be helpful in identifying areas of imbalance. Pick a day every month to sit down with one of these stones, and hold it in your hand as you feel all distractions and subconscious influences fade. When you have reached a place of peace and clarity, think about the effort you have given to your career, romantic relationships, friendships, family, health, and personal development over the past month. Have you been putting in long hours at work while ignoring your basic health needs, or have you been so focused on your significant other that you've forgotten to maintain your friendships? Be honest and objective in your assessment. Libra makes decisions based on the evidence presented, and if you are aware of how much energy you are giving to different areas of your life, you can manage and blend them more effectively.

MINDFUL MEDIATOR

Relationship-focused Libra draws our attention to our partnerships and shows us how to navigate challenges with one another in the spirit of unity. If problems arise with your partner, placing two pieces of rose quartz, ametrine, or any love-related stone in your bedroom or around your home can invite in the energy of pairs and create a more harmonious atmosphere between you and your significant other. If communication breaks down, kindly ask your partner to write a wish for the relationship, along with a constructive solution, and place it under one of the stones; then write yours and place it under the remaining stone. After the two wishes have sat for a day, come back to review them together. Do you both still feel that these are areas that require improvement? In what ways are they connected? Be respectful of the other's perspective. Negotiations may prove more fruitful when the conversation isn't as emotionally charged and challenges are approached with objectivity. This ritual can also be performed solo: write an intention for bringing beauty and love into your life, along with an actionable solution, and place it under rose quartz for twenty-four hours; then, hold the stone to your heart and assess whether the solution is something you want to pursue.

SCORPIO

October 23–November 21

Symbol
THE SCORPION

Quality
FIXED

Element
WATER

Ruling Planet
PLUTO, MARS

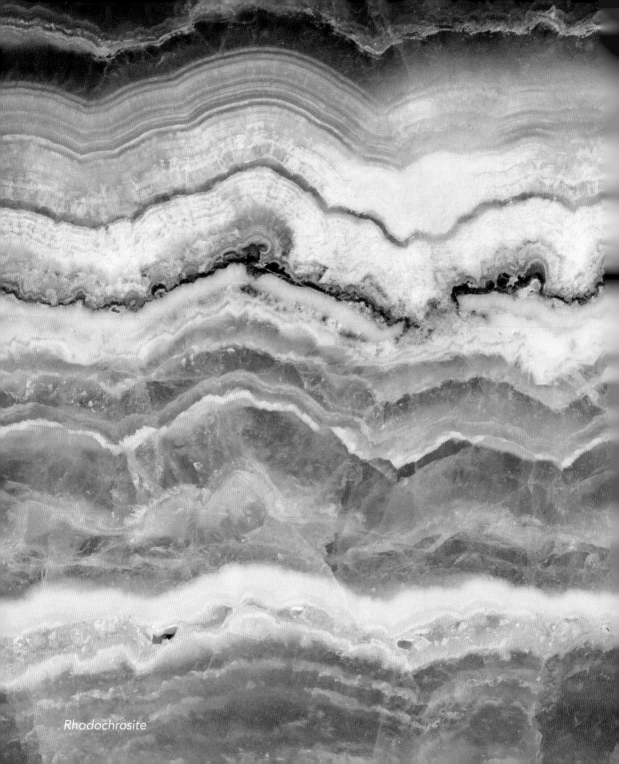

Rhodochrosite

Scorpio may be a water sign, but fire flows through its veins. Symbolized by the Scorpion, this intense and mysterious sign represents radical transformation and powerful cycles of death and rebirth. Piercing through all that is superficial, the Scorpion strikes at the rawest, most intimate parts of the soul to reveal its hidden depths and unlock its true potential. This process can feel poisonous, as some parts of ourselves seem to perish, but this is the magic of Scorpio's venom. This potent energy purges what no longer serves us so that what remains can prevail. Like the phoenix, Scorpio seemingly burns to ash, only to remerge ten times stronger.

When we channel the energy of this sign, the extreme experiences we face and the strength of our emotions allow us to transform on a profound level. Concerned with the truth, Scorpio plunges into the shadows we would prefer to keep secret, knowing that the only way out of the darkness is through it. This probing energy prompts us to delve into the deepest parts of our soul in order to access our untapped power. So, what do we find when we search our subconscious? Who are we, scars and all? By journeying with Scorpio energy, we are able to ask ourselves these difficult questions and finally confront the answers simmering below the surface.

When we encounter situations that push us past our limits and expose our vulnerabilities, we instinctively call upon Scorpio energy. These moments of intense pressure or hardship give us no choice but to take on a new form, and Scorpio energy provides the strength we need to carry ourselves through to the other side. A true survivor in every sense of the word, Scorpio recognizes that a breaking point is a powerful opportunity for rebirth.

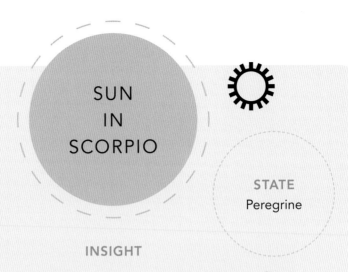

SUN
IN
SCORPIO

STATE
Peregrine

INSIGHT

Emotions are like water, so let them flow. The more you try to repress them, the more overwhelming they become.

Some people fear the dark, but not the mysterious Scorpion. In fact, exploring the hidden depths of the human psyche is what you're all about. Understanding what makes people tick interests you, as does peeling back the superficial layers of your interactions. Your ability to connect the dots and distill the truth comes from your powerful intuition and magnetic presence, which grant you excellent foresight and greater control over your environment. A formidable opponent, you typically predict others' moves with ease and maneuver yourself accordingly. Your gift for cunning, long-term strategy typically leads to success in business, but when you apply this degree of calculation to your interpersonal relationships others may find you controlling or overbearing.

RHODOCHROSITE

USE FOR: EMOTIONAL RESPONSIBILITY, AWARENESS, MUTUAL RESPECT, EMPATHY

COLOR
Raspberry pink to rose red with delicate swirling or banding

CHAKRA
Heart

MANTRA
I see beauty in everyone and everything around me.

The radiant color of rhodochrosite represents selfless love, positivity, and compassion. Excellent for relationships, this stone gently brings irrational fears and destructive habits to the surface, allowing them to be released. Rhodochrosite teaches your heart to grow by casting aside fear-based thinking and judgments so you can love yourself, and others, fully and freely.

RITUAL: Carry rhodochrosite in your pocket or wear it on your body for an entire day as a reminder to continuously shine love on yourself and your interactions. If you see your reflection in a mirror, say something positive about yourself. If you notice a colleague doing impressive work, compliment the person. If your significant other is excited about a new project or career development, show your support. When you approach every encounter as an opportunity to bring more love into the world, life naturally feels brighter.

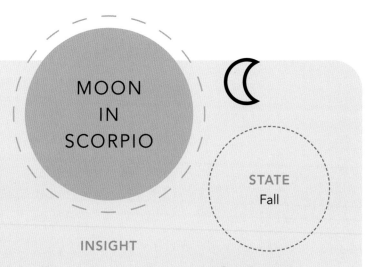

MOON
IN
SCORPIO

STATE
Fall

INSIGHT

For wrongs that cannot be rectified and events beyond your control, the best remedy is often release, not retribution.

Your emotional well runs deeper than most. Behind your seemingly quiet exterior lies a hotbed of smoldering passion and intensity. When you love, you love with every fiber of your being, and when you hurt, the pain cuts you at your core. You are consumed by strong feelings that carry you to emotional extremes and render your world in black and white. Friend or foe, inner circle or outcast—there is no middle ground. Winning your affection requires an iron-clad level of commitment, and you may repeatedly test those closest to you to confirm their loyalty. Those who pass will gain you as a lifelong confidant, but those who fail should prepare for quite the sting! With your zero-tolerance policy for lying or betrayal, any attempts to deceive or slight you will surely provoke your vengeful side.

CELESTITE

USE FOR: INNER PEACE, HONEST COMMUNICATION, PURITY, HARMONY

COLOR
Soft, glacial blue

CHAKRA
Throat

MANTRA

*I feel fully at peace
with the present.*

Calming and nourishing, celestite feels like a life preserver on an emotionally turbulent sea. The gentle energy of this stone holds you steady as you navigate rugged obstacles and distracting environments. If you feel overwhelmed by your emotions, reach for this stone and be rocked back to comfort and safety by its soothing, lullaby-like quality.

RITUAL: Regain composure in emotionally charged moments by cooling down with celestite. When stressed, grieving, or angry, hold this stone in your hand and gaze upon its delicate, sky-blue hue as you are transported to a place of tranquility. Focus on your breath and envision yourself wading into a crystal-clear ocean as you slowly count down from ten to zero. With each step forward, visualize the cooling water around you carrying away unpleasant sensations and feelings in soft waves. Using this exercise to unwind and uplift can prevent you from spiraling downward into negative thoughts.

ASCENDANT
IN
SCORPIO

INSIGHT

Sensing threats in your environment is healthy, but assuming threats are present can be isolating.

Quiet and mysterious, you come across as an enigmatic but powerful individual. Your keen intuition functions like a sixth sense, giving you the ability to guess what others are feeling. Because of your natural magnetism, you are able to get close to people quickly, though you typically keep your thoughts and feelings to yourself. Careers that involve in-depth strategy or research allow you to shine, and you excel in fields that require you to solve one problem over a long period of time, such as law, therapy, or investigative work. Depending on who you're with and what your motives are, you can be secretive or direct, charming or standoffish, making it difficult for people to pin down who you really are. While your highly perceptive nature allows you to avoid many pitfalls, your suspicions of others' intentions can become excessive if left unchecked.

SMOKY QUARTZ

USE FOR: CALMNESS, PROTECTION, CLEANSING, POSITIVITY

COLOR
Light grayish brown to deep black

CHAKRA
Root

MANTRA

I let go of fear and move forward with positivity.

Kick negativity to the curb with the detoxifying properties of smoky quartz. This stone diffuses jealousy, fear, and anger as it softly grounds the emotional body. Smoky quartz acts as first aid for old emotional wounds and past trauma, and can be used to settle any uncomfortable thoughts or feelings that begin to surface.

RITUAL: Let light into the windows of your heart with a morning meditation. On a sunny day, find a quiet and comfortable place outside and sit down. Hold smoky quartz in your hand and close your eyes as you focus on the feeling of sunlight on your skin. Connect to the purifying energy of your stone and envision shadows lifting from your toes all the way to the top of your head. Concentrate on the warmth of the sun filling your body with light until you feel completely weightless, then open your eyes. Greet the day with joy and soak in the beauty around you. Promptly store smoky quartz away from sunlight to prevent fading.

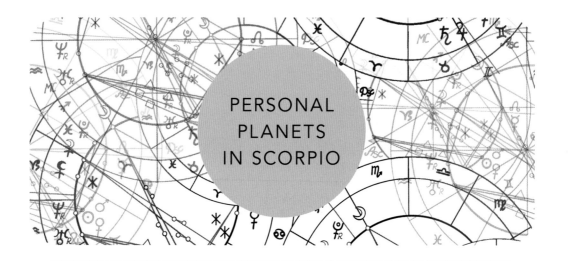

VENUS IN SCORPIO

STATE
Detriment

INSIGHT

*You can learn to show vulnerability in stages.
Open up about easier topics first to get more
comfortable with sharing deeper feelings later on.*

There's love, and then there's Scorpio love. This can be a tricky placement, as your longing for intense intimacy is at odds with your highly guarded emotions. You want to let others in but have difficulty relinquishing control and showing vulnerability. Connecting with your partner on a deeply personal level is crucial to you, as you seek to enmesh with their mind, body, and soul. Once someone gains your trust, you give 100 percent in your commitments and won't hesitate to fight for the ones you love. While this makes you a fiercely loyal lover, your extremely protective nature can border on controlling. When doubts or fears surface, meditating with kunzite, a stone of emotion and release, can break down the walls around your heart and allow you to be more open and trusting.

MERCURY IN SCORPIO

STATE
Peregrine

INSIGHT

Keep your opinions flexible. You can miss out on potential opportunities and beneficial connections if you form rigid or snap judgments.

Direct and forceful in communication, you have an all-or-nothing mind-set— and your sharp opinions can have a polarizing effect. You also want to get to the bottom of things, to an almost obsessive degree. Uncovering the truth drives your thought processes, whether you are dissecting a person's real motives or poking holes in an opponent's argument. You love probing others' minds for hidden secrets. Wear black tourmaline, a harmonizing and purifying stone, to curb prying tendencies or the need to analyze flaws.

MARS IN SCORPIO

STATE
Domicile

INSIGHT

Pay attention to what motivates you. Consider ways to align personal objectives with those that benefit a larger community.

This is a highly potent placement with immense drive, endless power, and unri-valed sexual magnetism. With your all-or-nothing attitude, you only delve into work that you are passionate about and that pushes your boundaries. Forceful, unyielding, and sometimes ruthless in pursuit of a goal, you don't let anything stop you from getting what you want. Though your relentless energy gives you incredible staying power and leadership qualities, you can be inflexible or hostile when forced to follow orders. Keeping Apache tears, gently supportive stones, at work can ease aggression and encourage peaceful conflict resolution.

THREADS OF TRANSFORMATION

The perceptive Scorpion pierces through facades to release the deeply ingrained beliefs, patterns, and behaviors blocking its transformation. By connecting to Scorpio energy, we learn to identify and let go of hidden sources of negative energy lodged in our subconscious. A cord-cutting ritual is an excellent way to separate toxicity and tension from the body and mind. Hold smoky quartz, black tourmaline, or any detoxifying stone in your hand with your eyes closed as you focus on your breath for five minutes. Afterward, notice any areas of your body that still feel tight, heavy, or sluggish. Concentrate on the specific sensation in each, and listen to the messages that accompany it. For instance, if your chest or heart is heavy, do you feel unworthy of love? If your throat or neck is tight, do you feel insecure in communication? After reflecting, visualize a cord being drawn out from each point of tension, along with any negative self-talk or limiting thoughts that surface, such as "I am unworthy of love." Finally, use your stone to trace around your body as you cut through each cord. The physical act of pulling energetic blockages away from the body and slashing through disparaging statements is a powerful declaration of your transformation.

FIERCE DEFENDER

With its sharp stinger and tough exterior, Scorpio is highly protective when it comes to love, but being guarded isn't always a bad thing. In fact, many encounters call us to fiercely defend our heart. To protect your heart against negative influences, unwanted advances, or toxic connections, place palo santo, loose incense, or any protection-related herbs (rosemary, bay leaves, etc.) in a pot on a nonflammable surface. If you are sensitive to smoke or only have access to rooms with limited ventilation, perform this ritual outdoors. Surround the outside of the pot with kunzite, rhodochrosite, black tourmaline, and Apache tears, and light the contents of the pot as you repeat the following mantra: "My heart is protected and safe. No harm or danger may draw near." Allow the materials in the pot to fully burn to ash, then place black tourmaline and Apache tears by your front door, and place kunzite and rhodochrosite in your bedroom. Finally, smudge the ash on any doorways that lead into your home and windows for added protection.

SAGITTARIUS

November 22–December 21

Symbol
THE ARCHER

Quality
MUTABLE

Element
FIRE

Ruling Planet
JUPITER

Pyrite

Free-spirited and philosophical, Sagittarius was born to wander. Symbolized by the Archer, this sign is depicted by a centaur holding a bow and arrow that stretches toward the sky, representing expansion and higher learning. On its eternal quest for wisdom, Sagittarius covers tremendous distances as it travels around the world, always reaching for the next adventure. This sign thinks in broad strokes, dreams big, and seeks to unify the individual experiences it gathers to arrive at a greater understanding of the universe.

When we connect to Sagittarius energy, our personal views take on a more global and spiritual perspective as we align with a higher goal or truth. Under the independent and intellectual Archer, we search for knowledge and experiences that offer us a conscious direction in life and provide enlightenment on our path forward. With its boundless optimism, Sagittarius knows no limits to what it can learn or how far it can go, propelling itself with pure faith and positivity.

By channeling the energy of this sign, we gain a broader mentality and an openness that connects us to a larger purpose. Sagittarius teaches that a mind clear of judgments and inhibitions is required if we are to think and act with absolute freedom. When we fully believe in ourselves instead of the self-imposed boundaries that often restrict us, we are able to pursue objectives that serve our grandest visions and let our happiness flourish. While throwing caution to the wind may be difficult for some, the unbridled spirit of the Archer is able to move past fear and operate with confidence and enthusiasm wherever it goes. Ultimately, this attitude of abundance is what sets Sagittarius free, and its energy calls us to take over the reins of our own destiny and enjoy every moment of its wild ride.

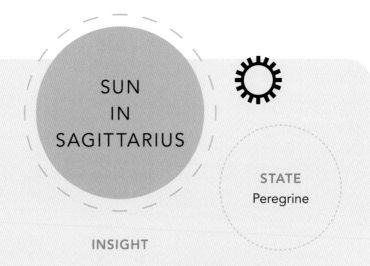

SUN
IN
SAGITTARIUS

STATE
Peregrine

INSIGHT

Big dreams require even bigger plans.
Start making them today.

For the inquisitive Archer, adventure is always on the horizon. Fueled by wanderlust and hungry for knowledge, you are drawn to opportunities for expansion, growth, and learning. While some people seek new experiences for their novelty, you enjoy them on a deeper level and value their ability to broaden your perspective. Philosophical pursuits that enrich your understanding of humanity or spirituality typically lead to frequent travel as your curiosity carries you around the globe. Whether journeying to a foreign country or exploring a nearby neighborhood for the first time, you are delighted by constant change and fill your life with fresh people and places. Though your desire for growth grants you a flexible outlook, you may find it difficult to operate within set boundaries and accept limitations due to your lofty optimism and need for absolute freedom. Assessing your aspirations with a discerning eye can prevent you from going to extremes.

LAPIS LAZULI

USE FOR: GUIDANCE, STUDYING, PROTECTION, PURPOSE

COLOR
Deep royal blue, either solid or dusted
with golden specks of pyrite

CHAKRA
Throat, third eye

MANTRA

*I know, see, and speak
the truth.*

A stone of truth and wisdom, lapis lazuli
is the quintessential compass for finding one's higher calling. Self-awareness
and purpose come into focus as the
activating energies of this stone support
learning and spiritual enlightenment.
In your search for greater understanding and depth, lapis lazuli guides you
toward a conscious path of authentic
self-expression and profound insight.

RITUAL: Clarify your direction when you
feel lost by going deep with lapis lazuli.
Lie down and meditate with this stone on
your forehead; close your eyes, and feel
lapis lazuli's peaceful energy leading you
to a state of total openness and awareness. When you've quieted your mind,
envision in front of you a door to your
past. Open it and walk through, making
only objective observations. After a few
minutes, visualize a doorway that leads
to the present; walk through it, making
additional observations. Finally, visualize
a door that leads to your future. What do
you see when you cross the threshold?
Having a clear direction in life requires a
strong vision of the future you desire, but
to know where you want to go you must
first understand where you've been and
where you are now. View your journey in
its entirety to find the answers within.

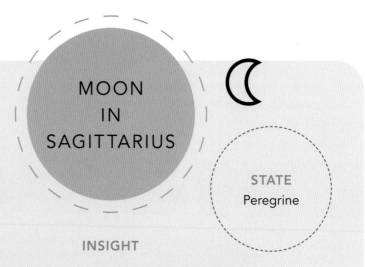

MOON IN SAGITTARIUS

STATE
Peregrine

INSIGHT

Reflection is enriched by patience. The full value of your experiences can only be gleaned when you aren't rushing toward the next one.

The sky's the limit when it comes to your inner world. This placement bestows you with boundless optimism and a perpetual sense of wonder. Adventurous and expansive, you need freedom to thrive, both mentally and physically—any attempts to fence you in feel stifling. The situations and connections that make you feel most comfortable are ones that allow you to come and go without restriction. While this detached air can be interpreted as disinterest, you are simply open: your naturally cheerful disposition makes it hard for anything to get under your skin, and every obstacle is a lesson to learn from. However, your tolerance and generosity may quickly dissolve when people display insular or narrow-minded thinking. If your work or relationships have no room for potential or change, you will find fulfillment challenging.

OBSIDIAN

USE FOR: HEALING, PROTECTION, ANCHORING, REALITY CHECK

COLOR
Translucent dark brown or black

CHAKRA
Root

MANTRA

*I am grounded in my
personal power.*

The regulating properties of obsidian provide support and stability during change. With this stone, scattered thoughts are reined in and imbalances are released. When the promise of a new exploit presents itself and impulsivity begins to brew, use this stone to find your center before you're swept off your feet.

RITUAL: Balance your perspective by slowing down with obsidian in a morning meditation. After you wake up, sit on the floor with both feet flat on the ground (not tucked underneath) and hold this stone in your left hand. Focus on your inhale and exhale as you notice your breath begin to fall into a gentle, steady rhythm. After five minutes, gaze into the dark color of your stone as you feel it draw out negativity and shadow tendencies from the base of your spine, until all restlessness and pressure have dissipated. Beginning your day with this practice helps to curb indulgent or spontaneous behavior by releasing excess energy and grounding your physical body.

ASCENDANT IN SAGITTARIUS

INSIGHT

Look toward the stars but keep your feet on the ground—your idealistic visions are best executed when they have a practical foundation.

Full of brazen opinions and fiery gusto, you come off as an enthusiastic explorer launching your next big adventure—but as swiftly as you arrive, you may depart. Frequent travel and activities keep you consistently on the move. This brings a touch-and-go feeling to your connections. More structured and scheduled types may find making plans with you difficult, but those closest to you understand that you must be free to roam. Your strong independence extends not only to your relationships but to your overall lifestyle and way of thinking. As a result, you may periodically change homes, careers, and hobbies as you strive to align with a higher purpose. Without a clear direction in life, your motivation and staying power can be relatively short-lived, but connected to your greater path, you can manifest your wildest dreams.

BRONZITE

USE FOR: CONSISTENCY, RESPONSIBILITY, PERSEVERANCE, CONFIDENCE

COLOR
Golden brown, sometimes greenish brown, with bronze inclusions

CHAKRA
Root, sacral

MANTRA

*I am deliberate
in my actions.*

Known as the stone of focused action and stone of courtesy, bronzite is all about follow-through and composure. The harmonizing energy of this stone teaches that abundance and success are attainable when thoughts are matched with action, making it a perfect companion for spiritual pursuits or career objectives. Rise to your challenges with bronzite and transform your dreams into reality.

RITUAL: Meditate with bronzite once a week, during the evening, to consistently check in with your intentions and progress. Before bed, place this stone on your desk and allow its boosting energy to clear your mind of doubt and insecurities while filling you with confidence. Then think of a current goal and jot down the basic steps needed to complete it. Be specific. For instance, if your goal is to meditate more, your first steps could be deciding how many times a week you want to meditate, marking the days on your calendar, and scheduling reminders on your phone thirty minutes prior to your sessions. When you check in the following week, assess how you did and note ways you can improve. By creating a plan and setting periodic check-ins, you support your goals with a clear, defined strategy.

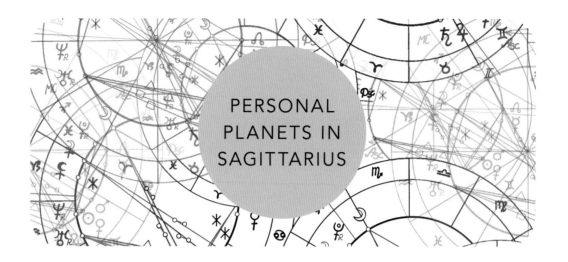

VENUS IN SAGITTARIUS

STATE
Peregrine

INSIGHT

Maintaining the connections that matter to you requires consistent effort. Scheduling some date nights in advance can make your partner feel like a priority.

Wild at heart, you are free-spirited in romance and aren't quick to settle down. Heavy commitments or clinginess can make you flighty or fickle; when given plenty of space, however, you are a loyal lover. Your ideal partner is a copilot who can accompany you on all your adventures and respects your freedom to roam. Though many are attracted to your higher plane of thinking, you often seem mentally preoccupied and may come off as callous or uncaring. Keeping pyrite, a stone of willpower and strength, in your bedroom can remind you that the practical aspects of a partnership deserve attention and must be tended to periodically.

MERCURY IN SAGITTARIUS

INSIGHT

Keeping an open mind involves acknowledging one's own blockages. Listening to critiques instead of swiftly dismissing them can prompt deeper introspection.

STATE
Detriment

Focused on the bigger picture, you enjoy discussions of broader subjects and larger concepts that add to your vast well of knowledge. Casual chitchat and mundane topics hold little interest for you, and you won't hesitate to voice your opinions. People appreciate your enthusiasm and sincerity, but your optimism can blind you to your own shortcomings at times. Wearing or carrying blue topaz, a stone of conscious communication, promotes self-control and self-awareness when expressing your viewpoint.

MARS IN SAGITTARIUS

INSIGHT

Slowing down and being more selective about where you spend your energy can drastically improve your follow-through.

STATE
Peregrine

Spontaneous and vigorous, you act in the moment and have great bursts of energy when inspiration hits. Your restless and instinctive drives seek out hands-on experiences and are stimulated by the unknown. Always on the go, you excel at extending into new territory and making quick decisions but aren't as well equipped to handle small details or nuances. Meditating with turquoise, a stone of serenity and empathy, adds a degree of sensitivity and finesse to round out any blunt or harsh edges.

WILD WANDERLUST

The nomadic Archer seeks greater knowledge and understanding from the experiences it gathers in the outside world. By attuning to the expansive energy of Sagittarius, we learn to widen our perspective by moving past preestablished boundaries and venturing into the unknown. If you feel stagnant or stuck in life, switching up your routine by exploring a new location can revitalize the spirit. Gather lapis lazuli, turquoise, or any stone of wisdom or truth, and pull up a map of your neighborhood or city on your phone before closing your eyes. Hold your stone to your forehead to access your intuition and higher consciousness as you deeply inhale and exhale ten times. With your eyes still closed, let your finger guide you to a point on the map before opening them to reveal your next destination. Travel there as soon as you can; if it's too far away, repeat the process on a smaller portion of the map. Using this practice to spur movement into new surroundings can facilitate growth and renew inspiration.

ROCK TO THE RHYTHM

Active and adaptable, Sagittarius is all about mobility and freedom when it comes to romance. Since Sagittarius rules the hips, a great way to get in touch with our sensuality and allow our energy to flow is by connecting to our body through dance. Put on a song you've never heard before and hold bronzite or obsidian at the base of your spine or pyrite above your navel to release inhibitions as you repeat the mantra, "My inner fire is fearless. Today, I ignite my soul." Let your body react to the music as it wants to. As you continue to dance, you can repeat the mantra aloud or in your head, imagining a fire in your belly brightening as it burns away any attachments that prevent beauty and love from coming into your life. Through the spontaneous movement of dance we become more flexible, open, and attuned to the natural rhythms of the universe and to our own primal energy. This physical movement can not only loosen emotional or mental blockages that prevent us from love but also promote independent expression.

CAPRICORN

December 22–January 19

Symbol
THE SEA GOAT

Quality
CARDINAL

Element
EARTH

Ruling Planet
SATURN

Green Tourmaline

Where there's a will, there's a way, and Capricorn is here to prove it. Symbolized by the Sea Goat—and commonly referred to as simply the Goat—this ambitious earth sign represents mastery of the physical world, and is characterized by steely grit and a relentless drive to achieve. As the first sign of winter, Capricorn must face the harsh realities of rugged weather and rely on its inner fortitude to carry it through the cold and dark nights ahead. Though the journey of the Goat is a long, difficult, and somewhat solemn one, Capricorn overcomes the greatest obstacles of its environment to reach the summit of success.

A master of self-control, the Goat can move mountains but also traverse the highest peaks through continued effort and focus over time. No stranger to hard work, Capricorn is measured and deliberate in everything it does, using structure and discipline as tools to steadily advance its goals. When we channel Capricorn energy, we are responsible and mature in our decisions, choosing to structure our lives for long-term success and rise to the challenges we encounter along the way.

When we connect to the energy of this sign, we tackle seemingly insurmountable tasks with patience and perseverance. This sign rarely loses its footing, and its energy pushes us to new levels of endurance, both mentally and physically. When our current path is a demanding uphill climb, Capricorn energy strengthens our resolve and won't let us stop until we've reached the top. Never one to shy away from duty or obligation, the indomitable Capricorn spirit transforms our biggest hardships into our greatest rewards, knowing that the struggles we experience are what ultimately lead us to prevail. In the end, the only way to go is up.

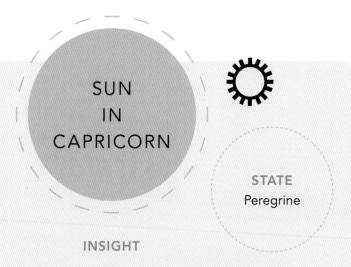

SUN
IN
CAPRICORN

STATE
Peregrine

INSIGHT

Scheduling days off from work ensures that you take the breaks you need to recharge. Spend this time with the people you care about and prioritize your health.

With great power comes great responsibility, and the disciplined Goat is ready for both. Highly ambitious with formidable focus, your persona is characterized by a steely resolve and a powerful drive to succeed. You understand that remarkable accomplishments require effort, sacrifice, and discipline, and you are willing to go the distance to reach the pinnacle of public achievement. This inner fortitude is perhaps your greatest strength, as your ability to drive through impossible obstacles makes you a relentless force at work and a rock-solid anchor for loved ones. While your unwavering commitment to your goals is inspiring, you are prone to working yourself to the point of exhaustion and neglecting your basic needs. Learning to nourish your body, maintain balance, and cultivate abundance within are your biggest lessons.

ONYX

USE FOR: SELF-DISCIPLINE, BALANCE, PURIFICATION, REGENERATION

COLOR
Deep black with white or gray banding

CHAKRA
Root

MANTRA

*I support and center myself
by releasing stress.*

The strength-giving properties of onyx make it a sturdy companion for physical and emotional support during times of stress or hardship. Protective and grounding, this stone prevents your personal energy from being drained and encourages wise decision making. Excellent for people in business and those who are self-employed, onyx encourages healthy egotism by reinforcing boundaries and prioritizing self-care.

RITUAL: Set powerful intentions for grounding and stability by meditating with onyx. When faced with a difficult task, sit on the floor and hold this stone in your hand with your eyes closed. Concentrate on your breath for two minutes as you feel negativity being drawn away from your body, then write on a small piece of paper a positive intention for tackling your current task, such as, "My intention is to feel calm and centered when I am frustrated." Afterward, fold your intention and place it under your stone near your workspace. The energy of onyx unfurls slowly over time, so keeping your intention beneath the stone will not only help it take root, but make it grow stronger each day.

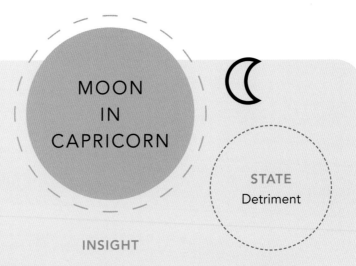

MOON IN CAPRICORN

STATE
Detriment

INSIGHT

Relinquishing control is just as powerful as exerting control. Showing your sensitivity allows others to get closer to the true you.

Associated with composure and restraint, this placement brings a controlled touch to your emotions along with the ability to compartmentalize them. You are in touch with your feelings but you keep them in check more easily than most. Being productive comforts you, so work is often a major source of fulfillment. The need to be respected and feel worthwhile in the public sphere is also a driving force that leads you to pursue prestigious work or high-powered positions. Because your inner landscape is efficient and organized, you may view messy or intense emotions as wasteful or frivolous. You handle your feelings in such a practical and efficient manner that others may mistake you for being calculating or cold when, in reality, you are quite sensitive. Allowing your feelings to naturally rise to the surface without judgment or restriction can make you more aware of your inner needs.

ROSE QUARTZ

USE FOR: INNER HEALING, COMPASSION, STRESS RELIEF, GENTLE SUPPORT

COLOR
Soft shades of light to medium pink

CHAKRA
Heart

MANTRA

I am in tune with my heart's true desires.

Known as the stone of universal love, rose quartz is the ultimate healer in matters of the heart. This stone's nurturing properties gently wash away feelings of negativity and harshness, and replace them with kindness and forgiveness. Working with this stone not only increases your capacity for compassion but also opens the heart to self-acceptance.

RITUAL: Use rose quartz to transform overly critical thoughts and self-limiting beliefs into affirmations of love and positivity. When you feel yourself getting caught up in negative self-talk, hold rose quartz over your heart for two minutes as you allow feelings of warmth and tenderness to embrace you. Afterward, write any remaining insecurities or harsh opinions of yourself as "I think" phrases, and replace them with compassionate "I am" statements. For instance, you could turn "I think I am a failure" into "I am a successful work in progress"; or transform "I think my work is horrible" into "I am evolving my craft to the best of my ability each day." When you take a moment to ease self-criticism and show compassion toward your development, flaws and all, you'll find that moving forward is much easier.

ASCENDANT
IN
CAPRICORN

INSIGHT

Be your biggest fan, instead of your worst critic. You'll find that a little self-love goes a long way.

Polished and competent, you make a respectable first impression with your authoritative presence. It's rare that you're not well put together, as you like to present yourself in a professional light. Highly aware of social mores, you have a dignified, almost formal quality that makes you appear serious or reserved. This isn't to say that you aren't capable of letting loose and having fun, but you prefer to keep a buttoned-up image in the public eye, along with a spotless reputation. Admired for your impressive work ethic and hard-earned achievements, you come across as a highly disciplined and ambitious individual who is focused on long-term success. Though your relentless drive allows you to accomplish much in your career, it can also produce immense pressure and heavy expectations. There's nothing wrong with setting high standards for yourself as long as you're also kind and forgiving in the process.

GREEN TOURMALINE

USE FOR: RENEWAL, COMPASSION, PATIENCE, BALANCE

COLOR
Light to dark shades of vivid grass green
or forest green

CHAKRA
Heart

MANTRA

*I hold myself
with tenderness.*

Healing and grounding, green tourmaline provides much-needed relief and restoration to an overworked system. If you've been burning the midnight oil, this stone is crucial for helping you unwind, as its opening energy gently releases stress and tension while instilling calm.

RITUAL: Unplug from work and connect to your heart by using green tourmaline in an evening meditation. Before bed, lay in a comfortable position with this stone over your heart and close your eyes. Focus on your breathing as you begin to shift your attention and energy from your head to the center of your chest, saying, "I open my heart" on the inhale and, "I quiet my mind" on the exhale. Repeat this for ten deep breaths. Afterward, listen for any messages that your heart may be trying to tell you in this receptive, loving state.

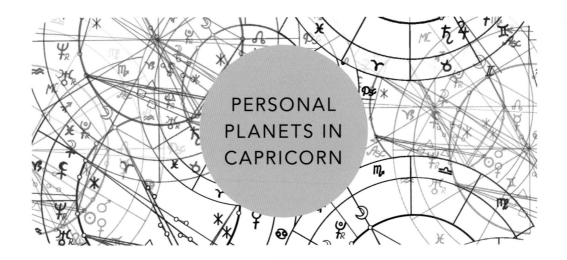

VENUS IN CAPRICORN

STATE
Peregrine

INSIGHT

Actions speak louder than words, but expressing your feelings out loud shows others that you care.

Logical and concerned with long-term success, you have a practical approach to love and are looking for someone who you can truly invest in. Because you value a measure of predictability and security in romance, you are careful when considering potential suitors and must make sure that they check off all the important boxes before fully committing. Once paired, you are a trusted and devoted lover who does not shy away from responsibility or hardship. With your realistic attitude toward love, you understand that difficulties inevitably arise in relationships, and you view them as natural concerns that can be worked through with effort. While your levelheaded outlook makes you a grounded partner, your constant "cool" may be interpreted as a lack of enthusiasm. Wearing garnet, a stone of revitalization, can bring more passion and sensuality to your love life.

MERCURY IN CAPRICORN

INSIGHT

Be confident in your words and speech. Your intelligence and preparedness will naturally shine through.

STATE
Peregrine

You are deliberate, precise, and goal-oriented in communication. Your conversations drive toward a definitive point, and may center around strategy or logistics until everything is set and understood. Your structured way of thinking is similarly methodical. This efficiency and clarity are assets in areas like policy, planning, and management but may come off as stiff or overly rigid in other contexts. Meditating with tree agate, a stone of inner peace, before presentations or important meetings can soothe nerves and boost confidence for enhanced charisma.

MARS IN CAPRICORN

INSIGHT

Don't defer your happiness to a later date. Find fulfillment in the present and appreciate what you already have.

STATE
Exaltation

You rise to meet any challenge. This powerful placement gives you an industriousness and unstoppable drive to achieve, making you a formidable force when it comes to work. You don't mind pulling an all-nighter at the office as long as it gets the job done, and you won't sacrifice quality or cut corners in the process either. But left unchecked your desire for productivity can border on workaholism. Place emerald, a stone of success and love with compassionate, regulating energies, on your desk to promote better work-life balance.

ULTIMATE TASKMASTER

No matter how challenging the terrain may be, the Goat never stops climbing. By tapping into the resilient energy of Capricorn, we learn to tackle our greatest obstacles head-on by employing structure and self-discipline that lead to success. To accomplish a large goal or difficult task, hold onyx, tree agate, or any grounding stone in your hand and sit on the floor with both feet flat on the ground. Concentrate on your breath for five minutes as you begin to feel increasingly anchored to the earth. Afterward, set your stone aside and write down the biggest or most uncomfortable task you currently face, then schedule a solid block of time during the week to work on it. Make sure this block is at least a few hours long and distraction-free. When faced with an unusually tough task, we may feel so daunted by the work required that we put it off or avoid it. However, when equipped with Capricorn's strength and willpower, we are able to prevail over any problem as long as we're willing to prioritize it and put in the effort.

ANCHOR TO THE EARTH

Strong and stable, Capricorn brings a grounded and practical perspective to love that can help us define our long-term goals or reassess the viability of our current connections. To set powerful intentions for your current romantic situation, meditate with rose quartz, garnet, or green tourmaline over your heart for five minutes and feel its nourishing, compassionate energy gently surround you. Think about the tangible progress you'd like to see, together with your ideal time intervals, whether the focus is dating, marriage, children, or simply reigniting your inner passion. Don't be afraid to be specific or think far ahead, as Capricorn energy thrives when plans and organization are involved. Afterward, write your intention on a piece of paper and bury it in the ground, preferably near a sturdy tree, for added support. If you are not able to bury it in soil, visualize performing the action in your mind instead. Connecting to the energy of Capricorn's earth element not only prompts us to reflect more seriously on the tangible aspects of our romantic goals, it also allows our intentions to remain firmly grounded.

AQUARIUS

January 20–February 18

Symbol
THE WATER BEARER

Quality
FIXED

Ruling Planet
URANUS, SATURN

Element
AIR

Amethyst

Expect Aquarius to fit the mold and they'll remake the entire machine. Symbolized by the Water Bearer, this progressive air sign is characterized by its revolutionary ideas and sharp intellect, as well as its humanitarian efforts. Concerned with the betterment of society as a whole, Aquarius represents innovation and collaboration, as its community-oriented objectives and forward-focused vision seek to create a brighter future for all. By fighting the status quo, the electric energy of Aquarius disrupts our systems and jolts us into entirely new ways of thinking.

When we connect to the energy of this sign, we are pushed away from familiar concepts toward shocking revelations that shake the foundation of our beliefs. The transformative Water Bearer asks us to dismantle the outdated conventions and social constructs preventing our evolution, and shed the oppressive and restrictive opinions that keep us segregated. When self-imposed limitations or complacency threaten our ability to grow and learn from others, the liberating energy of Aquarius moves us beyond our personal perspective and unites us with the collective consciousness. This sign believes that the world can be transformed into a place of fairness and tolerance if we work together, and its spirit calls us to be a part of this positive, global change.

Under the influence of Aquarian energy, we set ego aside and focus on the group. The Water Bearer teaches that we're all a part of a larger community, whether it's a family, neighborhood, or the planet itself. Ultimately, Aquarius challenges us to think more deeply about the human condition and how we can share lessons effectively: when we're equipped with this larger, universal knowledge, we can find solutions that benefit us all.

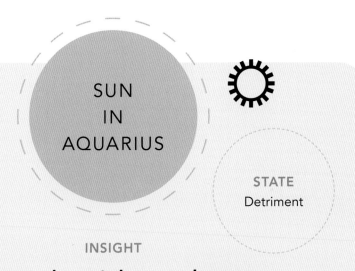

SUN
IN
AQUARIUS

STATE
Detriment

INSIGHT

Change doesn't have to happen immediately. Trade spontaneity for foresight—your future self will thank you.

For the rebellious Water Bearer, rules are meant to be broken. Constantly challenging outdated conventions and old ways of thinking, you march to the beat of your own drum and encourage others to do the same. Though this placement appears to imply challenges in expressing your identity, it merely emphasizes that you excel at deviating from the norm. While the sun is associated with the expression of one's ego, you develop your identity by distancing yourself from your ego and prioritizing collective concerns. Your personality can seem a bit abstract or even paradoxical at times, as your interests tend to be more group oriented than intimate or personal. Though your unusual outlook fuels your originality, your desire to set yourself apart from others can drive you to adopt polarizing positions or opinions. Connect to your intuition to balance your views so your vision and intentions remain clear.

AMETHYST

USE FOR: POSITIVE TRANSFORMATION, GUIDANCE, INNER PEACE

COLOR
Pale lilac to deep purple

CHAKRA
Crown

MANTRA

I am receptive and open to the solutions the universe provides.

Filter out distractions and focus on the path ahead with the soothing energy of amethyst. Calming and balancing, this stone promotes clarity and peace of mind with its intuitive and stabilizing properties. By helping you operate from a place of openness and acceptance, this stone improves communication and boosts productivity by harmonizing joint efforts.

RITUAL: Seek realistic solutions by using amethyst to access your inner wisdom. If you are dealing with a particular problem, write a potential solution on a piece of paper. Afterward, hold this stone over your forehead for two minutes and allow its soothing presence to quiet your thoughts. When you are finished, review your initial solution—paying attention to whether it sounds rigid or narrow—then rework it so it is more flexible, moderate, or balanced. Finally, compare the two solutions and reflect on which will serve you and the people involved in the fairest and most effective way. Problem solving by creating multiple solutions at varying levels of action or intensity allows you to examine all sides of an issue before deciding how to move forward.

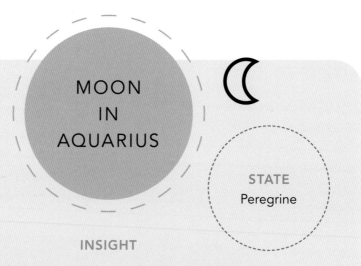

MOON IN AQUARIUS

STATE
Peregrine

INSIGHT

Explaining your unique means of processing emotions can help others feel closer to you.

Just because this placement is less emotional than other signs doesn't mean you lack feeling. In fact, connecting to others is important to you, though you tend to do so with a more objective perspective. Logic and reason appeal to you more than passion or sentimentality; you analyze feelings based on what "makes sense." Because of your intellectual take on emotions, you are not easily swayed by dramatic displays of affection or heated outbursts. You may have difficulty comprehending why others react impulsively or irrationally in certain situations. This ability to remain calm and levelheaded in any environment makes you extremely helpful during a crisis, but it may be mistaken for coldness or aloofness in romantic or interpersonal matters. Finding partners and friends who respect your need for space and appreciate the logical support you provide is key in fortifying your sense of community.

LARIMAR

USE FOR: STRESS RELIEF, COMPASSION, SENSITIVITY, PATIENCE

COLOR
Sea blue

CHAKRA
Throat

MANTRA

*I express myself
without inhibition.*

Like a calm ocean's waves, the intuitive energy of larimar gently flows, bringing head and heart into alignment. This stone encourages you to lean into your feelings and the wisdom they offer instead of justifying or rationalizing them. Use larimar to speak your personal truth, and you'll find that you can manifest in reality the emotional concepts you've been seeking to explain.

RITUAL: Locate areas of emotional blockages within your body by meditating with larimar. Hold this stone in your hands for one minute with your eyes closed as you breathe deeply. Imagine gentle water surrounding you as it cleanses and calms your thoughts, then touch the stone to your forehead, throat, and heart, lingering over each area for one minute. Pay attention to the sensations that arise and the differences between them. Do you feel more heaviness, tension, or sluggishness in one area than in another? If so, this could be an indication of an imbalance. For instance, if tension is present in your throat, ask yourself if you have been communicating your true feelings. Heightening awareness of your physical body helps you recognize and validate your emotions.

ASCENDANT IN AQUARIUS

INSIGHT

Your vision will go through many iterations before it is complete. Allow the changes to inspire you.

A bit of a rebel with a penchant for boundary pushing, you are seen as a visionary well ahead of the curve. Your forward-thinking spirit shines wherever innovation is concerned, giving you an extra edge in science, technology, and fashion, along with a strong digital presence. Because you are easily bored, you are quick to experiment with new styles and may alter your appearance frequently. You are often regarded as a trendsetter or creative genius with an exceptional ability to take risks and apply fresh ideas. Highly aware of collective social dynamics, you circulate among diverse groups of people and use your keen insight to benefit and connect various communities. Though your far-sighted vision comes across as highly intellectual and open to new ideas, you can surprise people with a stubborn streak when your authority is challenged. Listen to others' views without rushing to form an opinion to be a more effective leader.

HONEY CALCITE

USE FOR: RESPONSIBILITY, PERSISTENCE, LEADERSHIP, COURAGE

COLOR
Transparent pale yellow to medium gold

CHAKRA
Root, solar plexus, third eye

MANTRA

*I teach and lead
with respect.*

For challenges associated with change, honey calcite is the perfect remedy. This stone provides a boost of confidence, insight, and action to enhance motivation and decision making. Beneficial when you are developing a new skill, honey calcite increases receptivity to all types of learning and to instruction from others, even if it deviates from your typical preferred methods.

RITUAL: Think outside the box and gain a fresh perspective by using honey calcite in a mini reflection. Hold this stone in your hand and envision a golden light above you, casting aside the shadows and pulling you toward a brighter future. Once you feel light and uplifted, draw a square on a piece of paper. Write any self-limiting beliefs inside the square, then write positive intentions around the outside of the shape. When you are finished, cross out the words inside the square, one at a time, as you repeat aloud the following: "I release what no longer serves me." Keep this paper near the mirror in your bathroom. Remembering what you actively choose to leave behind and what you are deliberately moving toward is a powerful tool for introspection that can help solidify new habits, patterns, and positive change.

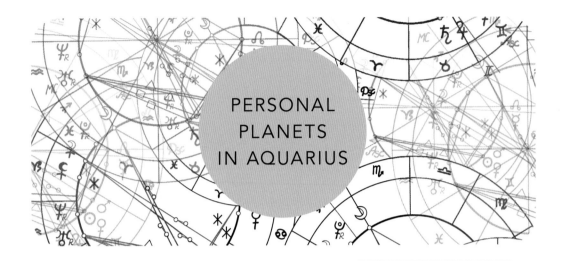

VENUS IN AQUARIUS

STATE
Peregrine

INSIGHT

Emotional displays are not always just for show.
Indulge a partner who is being affectionate
and appreciate the special moments.

When it comes to romance, you lead with your head rather than your heart. You have a detached and unconventional approach to love in which almost anything goes, as long as you're given plenty of space. Freedom and mental stimulation are prerequisites for forming a lasting relationship with you, and your appreciation of congenial company may lead to blurred lines between romantic love and friendship. Though your originality and inventiveness are attractive, partners may find that your abstract thoughts carry you out of reach at times. Placing sugilite, a stone of passion and devotion, in the southern area of your room can bring warmth and affection to your relationship, sparking the exchange of ideas between you and your loved one.

MERCURY IN AQUARIUS

INSIGHT

Share your wisdom without being patronizing. Your insights are best received when others feel like they can relate to you.

This placement bestows a mental prowess that is hard to match. You process information quicker than most, and combine logic and intuition to find ingenious solutions to complex problems. Though your thought patterns may confound most people, your unorthodox methods produce results. Overconfidence may lead to a sense of superiority if left unchecked. Wearing angelite, a stone of compassion and wholeness, can encourage greater understanding and forgiveness in communication. Note: angelite is water soluble; do not get it wet.

STATE
Exaltation

MARS IN AQUARIUS

INSIGHT

Your creativity is your greatest ally in getting what you want. Constructing as many win-win partnerships as possible inevitably leads to success.

Fixed in some of your approaches yet fluid in others, you may act in ways that are unpredictable, eccentric, and even contrary. Driven by intellectual pursuits, you hold firmly to the goal at hand until a new wave of inspiration hits, spurring you to rapid transformation. Though this spontaneity can birth some of your greatest ideas, it may also make you prone to accidents or reinforce risky behavior. Rubbing hematite, a stone of grounding and protection, can prevent impulsive decision making.

STATE
Peregrine

AQUARIUS-INSPIRED RITUAL
RISE AND REFORM

The eccentric Water Bearer has no problem going off the beaten path, and its unconventional methods often lead to strokes of genius. By connecting to the inventive energy of Aquarius, we learn to break routine by experimenting with the fresh and unusual. To embrace a new perspective, use honey calcite, larimar, or angelite in a morning ritual. Upon rising, hold your stone in your hand for five minutes as you allow your mind to reach a state of total openness. Afterward, think of ways to switch up your morning routine. For instance, if you check your phone as soon as you wake up, choose to wait twenty minutes before looking at it; or, if you typically skip breakfast, make an effort to throw something together before work. Deviating from what you'd normally do feels uncomfortable at first, but trying unusual alternatives can spur creativity in surprising ways.

COMMUNITY HEALING

A socially conscious sign, Aquarius loves on a greater, collective scale, and its energy encourages us to radiate compassion and tenderness to the communities we feel called to support. Set loving intentions for a group of people—whether friends, family, or the world at large—by meditating with amethyst, sugilite, or rose quartz over your heart for five minutes. Allow feelings of abundance, positivity, and warmth to flow within you as you visualize the person or group you want to heal. Once you have a clear image in mind, take a slow, deep inhale and, as you exhale, direct outward all the energy you have gathered as you say, "I send you my purest love and my deepest healing." Practicing distance healing for the collective prompts us to pause our personal focus and detach ourselves from our ego. By invoking this Aquarius energy, we are better able to tap into the wellspring of universal love that can be shared anytime, anywhere, with anyone.

PISCES

February 19–March 20

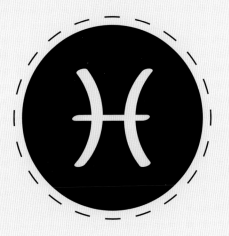

Symbol
THE FISH

Quality
MUTABLE

Element
WATER

Ruling Planet
NEPTUNE, JUPITER

Labradorite

The journey through the astrological wheel comes full circle in the compassionate water sign of Pisces. Symbolized by the Fish, Pisces is the final constellation in the sky, and signifies the culmination of a cycle as well as the transition to a new one. Endings and beginnings, the material and spiritual worlds, the conscious and the subconscious—the dual nature of Pisces represents the magical point between what we know and what remains to be seen, and its energy offers us a transcendent experience. Associated with dreams, imagination, and mystery, this sign blurs the boundaries between fantasy and reality, and dissolves the barriers that prevent us from truly merging with another.

As the last sign of the zodiac, Pisces embodies the lessons of all the signs that have come before it, which makes the Fish highly impressionable and empathetic. With a deep understanding of human nature, this sign relates easily to others and has a soft spot for those who are suffering or in need. Always willing to lend a helping hand or a patient ear, Pisces has a receptive energy that is free of judgment and creates a space of openness and acceptance where one can simply be.

By connecting to the energy of this sign, we tap into Pisces' boundless empathy and remarkable capacity for kindness. Under this energy, we learn to embrace the people and situations we encounter without expectations or assumptions, and give from the heart without reservation, knowing that the intimate bonds we form have the ability to heal the greatest wounds. By teaching us how to surrender to something bigger than ourselves, Pisces energy guides us toward a sense of oneness with the universe, a place where unconditional love leads to a realm beyond the self.

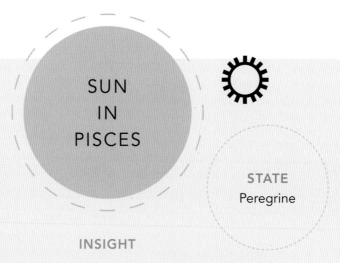

SUN IN PISCES

STATE
Peregrine

INSIGHT

Take time away to recharge without becoming reclusive. Too much isolation can slow your momentum and disconnect you from reality.

"Go with the flow" is the Fish's motto. Highly impressionable, you allow life's currents to carry you in whatever direction "feels right." An emotional and sensitive creature, you are guided by intuition rather than facts and have a wise, spiritual presence that seems otherworldly. There is no limit to your imagination, and you spend much of your time escaping through your dreams and fantasies. As a result of your heightened creativity, you give off an artistic, poetic vibe and frequently appear as though your head is lost in the clouds. This retreat into your own universe can provide a never-ending source of inspiration and enchantment, but it can also become a form of escapism or lead to disillusionment when the harsh realities of daily life begin to pile up. Cultivating balance and discipline are essential in establishing a sense of responsibility.

AQUAMARINE

USE FOR: INNER STRENGTH, COURAGE, STABILITY, STILLNESS

COLOR
Light bluish green

CHAKRA
Throat

MANTRA

*I harmonize
my mind and body.*

The regenerative properties of aquamarine are ideal for soothing and self-healing. Calming and strengthening, the energy of this stone is perfect for sensitive individuals who may have difficulty with focus or patience during meditation. If a task feels daunting or anxiety inducing, the tranquil presence of aquamarine can clear away confusion, worry, and stress.

RITUAL: Find balance and clarity through a weekly breath-work ritual. Start by sitting in an upright position with your head, neck, and back in a straight line. Hold aquamarine in your hand as you settle into a still posture, allowing your body to slowly relax and your thoughts to unwind. Then, shift your awareness to the sensation of air passing in and out of your nostrils. As your breath becomes smoother and deeper, focus on the cooling touch of air filling your nostrils on the inhale and the warm touch of air rushing past your nostrils on the exhale. If your attention drifts, grasp your stone as a gentle reminder to come back to the breath without judgment or criticism. Continue for five minutes, or until your inhale and exhale find a steady, rhythmic flow. Consciously balancing your physical breath can improve your mental and emotional balance as well.

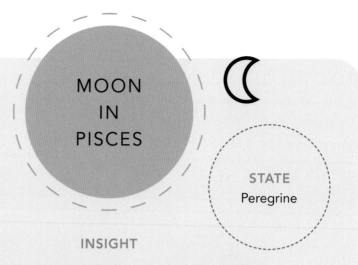

MOON
IN
PISCES

STATE
Peregrine

INSIGHT

You can control the outcome of a situation more easily than you think. Asserting your feelings and opinions will help you get what you want.

Highly attuned to the feelings of others, you are characterized by sensitivity, compassion, and depth. You soak up moods like a psychic sponge and have the uncanny ability to lower others' emotional defenses through genuine acceptance and understanding. Easily affected by human suffering, you are drawn to those in need and sometimes even dysfunctional individuals, who you seek to heal and help. Supporting and nurturing others may feel easier than caring for yourself: giving is second nature to you and fulfills you. Though your big heart is one of your greatest assets, you can become lost in the plight of others if you are not conscious about where you expend your energy. Using your strong intuition to assess people's intentions will help you discern between those who are sincere and those who have ulterior motives.

ARAGONITE STAR CLUSTER

USE FOR: EMOTIONAL STABILITY, ENDURANCE, PATIENCE, SELF-CONTROL

COLOR
Semitranslucent orange brown

CHAKRA
Root

MANTRA
I am an indomitable force.

Grounding and empowering, aragonite acts as a pillar of strength in times of doubt or hardship. When obstacles arise, this stone provides a boost of motivation and encouragement to meet challenges head-on. Hold onto this stone and feel its reassuring touch to remind you of your capabilities and to stand firm in your power.

RITUAL: To improve confidence, use aragonite in different placements around the home. Start by placing this stone in your bedroom, then move it to a different room or area in your home every week. When you see this stone, allow its warm, rich color to spark feelings of joy and optimism in your soul. Set an alarm on your phone to remind you when it's time to switch its location. Interacting with aragonite in multiple areas helps to spread its positive energy—the more you see it, the more it raises your spirits.

ASCENDANT
IN
PISCES

See the best in people but don't let their positive attributes blind you to their flaws—red flags shouldn't be ignored.

You have a soft, caring presence that makes a gentle and empathetic first impression. Naturally giving and selfless, you often take on the role of healer or counselor, as others frequently seek your company when they are troubled or stressed. Your exceptional listening skills combined with your soft-hearted personality make you an attentive and devoted friend who can always be depended upon in a crisis. Adapting to the energy of those around you, you instinctively know how to make others feel comfortable regardless of the circumstances. While others see you as an artistic, compassionate individual, you may also come across as naive or gullible when it comes to practical, real-world matters. Improving your sense of self-awareness and establishing boundaries is a vital self-care practice.

AMETHYST

USE FOR: BALANCE, WISDOM, CLARITY, STRESS RELIEF

COLOR
Pale lilac to deep purple

CHAKRA
Crown

MANTRA

I can align with my higher self when I tap into my intuition.

The cleansing and protective properties of amethyst regulate and balance emotions for a heightened state of consciousness. Purifying and stabilizing, this stone washes away lower energies that may be encouraging destructive patterns or behaviors even as it promotes clarity of mind. When facing a difficult decision, use this stone to access your inner wisdom for guidance.

RITUAL: Fortify your boundaries and improve sleep by using amethyst in an evening ritual. Before bed, wave this stone six inches away from your skin to remove negative energy accumulated throughout the day, then place the stone under your pillow or by the foot of your bed for a soothing slumber. The tranquilizing effects of amethyst alleviate nightmares, insomnia, and irritability for better-quality rest, and the protective properties of this stone shield you when you're energetically vulnerable.

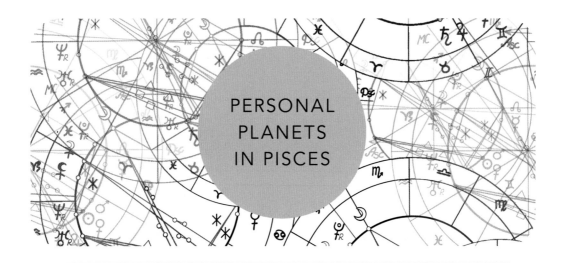

VENUS IN PISCES

STATE
Exaltation

INSIGHT

It's easy for you to lose yourself in another person. Learn the art of self-protection by setting healthy boundaries.

Your vision of love is nothing short of a fairy tale. You crave a transcendent, divine union where two souls unite as one and desire a partner who can fulfill your deep need for intimacy. Ethereal and elusive, you capture lovers' hearts with your entrancing presence and abundant emotional reservoir that never quits giving. Your sensitivity and generosity make you an incredibly compassionate partner, but some may take advantage of your kind and selfless nature if you are not careful. Wearing black tourmaline, a stone of grounding and protection, on your body can ward off the negative energy of those around you. Because this stone absorbs energy from others, cleanse it regularly by setting it under the light of the new or full moon.

MERCURY IN PISCES

STATE
Detriment

INSIGHT

Skirting an issue only delays the inevitable. Be up-front in the beginning to avoid complications down the line.

Your thoughts and communication are governed more by feeling and intuition than by logic. An emotional dreamer, you swim in a realm of endless possibilities, making it hard to pin you down to any one belief. Shying away from cold facts and specific details, your indirect manner and nebulous methods can seem disorganized, but what you lack in precision you make up for with imagination. Placing fluorite, a stone of clarity and balance, in your workspace can improve concentration and enhance decisiveness.

MARS IN PISCES

STATE
Peregrine

INSIGHT

Incorporating small routines into day-to-day life can anchor you in a consistent rhythm over time.

This is a more passive, gentle placement that floats with the current circumstances rather than trying to control them. Frequent changes in mood and energy may cause you to experience bursts of motivation followed by periods of inactivity, which can make structured work challenging. Flexible jobs that serve as an outlet for creative expression whenever inspiration strikes will benefit you the most. Holding labradorite, a stone of transformation, in a daily morning meditation, can free you from sluggish cycles by imparting the perseverance needed for positive change.

EXPLORING
THE DREAM WORLD

The ethereal Fish accesses the depths of its imagination by straddling the line between the material and spiritual realms. By invoking the otherworldly energy of Pisces, we learn to tap into our subconscious thoughts along with the creative magic that resides there. A great way to bridge the gap between our physical existence and transcendent experiences is through dream journaling. Keep a small notebook and pen or a tape recorder by your bed; before you sleep, hold amethyst, labradorite, or moonstone in your hand and feel its calming energy flow through you for one minute. When you are finished say, "I will remember my dreams when I wake," then set your crystal on a nightstand or by the foot of your bed to encourage deep slumber. Upon waking, immediately write down any dreams you had, paying attention to colors, shapes, and feelings that may have surfaced. Review them later in the day to distill their hidden meaning or at the end of the week for even greater insight. The meaning of your dreams may seem elusive at first, but noticing the images and symbols that recur can focus your intuition and guide you toward a greater sense of clarity.

FLOW AND FLOURISH

Compassionate and romantic, Pisces energy invites us to flow—and to heal ourselves—with its greatest power source: love. Let go of all that is preventing you from loving yourself wholly and unconditionally by using aquamarine, black tourmaline, or rose quartz in a shower ritual. Meditate with your crystal over your heart for one minute as you repeat aloud, "I am open to unconditional love" after every three breaths, then set the stone aside. As you shower, visualize a white light falling from your showerhead and illuminating the water around you until it glows bright, golden white. Allow the light to bathe you with its purifying energy, then envision every fear and doubt buried deep within being lifted gently to the surface of your body and washed down the drain. Notice how much lighter you feel when you are no longer carrying the attachments and burdens that obscure who you really are, a beautiful being deserving of immense love. By connecting to the element of water and aligning with this sign's gentle currents, we are able to dissolve the boundaries that prevent us from truly merging with others and find bliss in surrendering to a higher state of love.

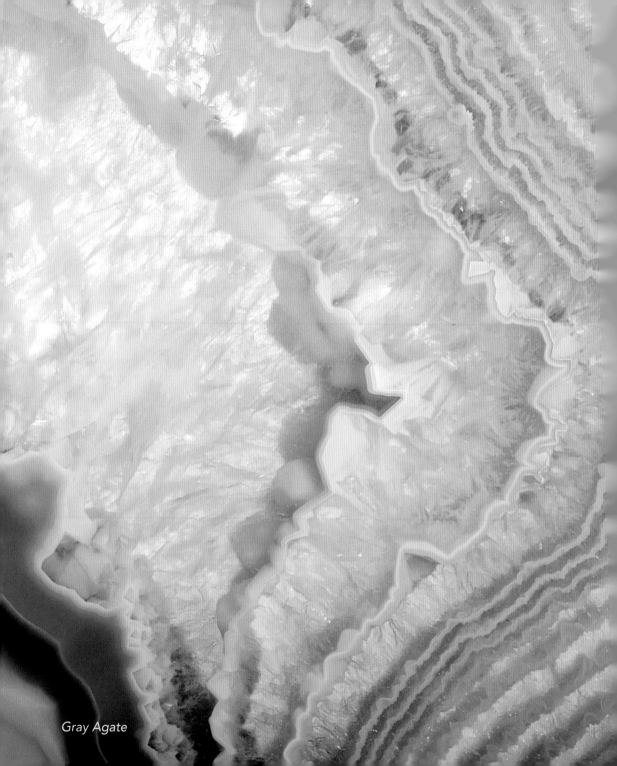
Gray Agate

BECOMING YOUR OWN GUIDE

Aristotle is quoted as saying, "Knowing yourself is the beginning of all wisdom." Traveling the path of self-discovery is perhaps the greatest journey of your lifetime. When cultivated with compassion, awareness, and patience, the relationship you have with yourself provides fertile ground for powerful change and healing. While astrology and crystals can help facilitate a deeper connection to the self, their overarching purpose is to serve as tools that allow you to become your own guide and source of wisdom. When combined, these resources reveal the first steps you can take toward illuminating your inner truth, enabling you to lead a conscious, intentional, and more fulfilling life.

As you move forward with a better understanding of what makes you *uniquely you*, remember that the stars are simply a mirror to the soul, reflecting your ability to shine to your brightest potential. Be open to the lessons of the universe, be gentle with your heart, and embrace the luminosity within.

GLOSSARY

AIR SIGN: Gemini, Libra, and Aquarius are air signs; these are characterized by intellect and communication.

ASCENDANT: Also known as the rising sign. It is the sign and degree rising on the eastern horizon at the moment of birth, with respect to the place of birth. The Ascendant represents the persona and image to the world.

CARDINAL SIGN: Aries, Cancer, Libra, and Capricorn are cardinal signs; these signs take initiative and action to exert control over their environment. They are the "starters" of the zodiac.

CHAKRA: An energetic focal point within the body believed to regulate various physical, mental, emotional, and spiritual processes. There are seven main chakras of the human body: root (base of spine), sacral (lower abdomen), solar plexus (upper abdomen), heart (center of chest), throat (over throat), third eye (between eyebrows), and crown (top of the head).

CHARGING: Also known as programming. The process of infusing a crystal with a specific energy, intention, or purpose, typically through meditation, a connection to the elements, or major celestial events. Charging a crystal restores the stone's ability to focus and channel energy.

CLEANSING: The process of releasing all previously accumulated or unwanted energy from a crystal.

DETRIMENT: The state of a planet when it is located in the sign opposite its rulership. The energy of the planet feels restricted here.

DIGNITY: A planetary state that describes a planet's comfort level and ease of expression in the sign where it is positioned. The most commonly used of the traditional essential dignities are: domicile, exaltation, detriment, and fall. A planet without any essential dignities is called a *peregrine* planet.

DOMICILE: Also known as rulership. The state of a planet when it is located in the sign that it rules over, or a planet's home position. The energy of the planet feels natural and comfortable here.

EARTH SIGN: Taurus, Virgo, and Capricorn are earth signs; they are characterized by stability and practicality.

ELEMENT: A component of nature; the four classical elements are fire, earth, air, and water. Each sign is associated with an element, which dictates the sign's basic temperament.

EXALTATION: The state of a planet when it is located in a sign similar in nature to the sign it rules. The energy of the planet feels refined and elevated here.

FALL: The state of a planet when it is located in the sign opposite its exaltation. The energy of the planet feels out of place here.

FIRE SIGN: Aries, Leo, and Sagittarius are fire signs; these signs are characterized by passion and enthusiasm.

FIXED SIGN: Taurus, Leo, Scorpio, and Aquarius are fixed signs. These signs are strong willed and focused. They are the "doers" or "builders" of the zodiac.

INNER PLANET: Also known as a personal planet. A planet with an orbit inside the asteroid belt (Mercury, Venus, and Mars) or, in astrology, a luminary (sun and moon). The inner planets in one's natal chart directly affect an individual's personality.

INTENTION: A purpose or aim that represents a commitment to carrying out an action or mind-set in the future.

LUMINARY: Also known as a light. The term "luminary" refers to the sun or moon, as both provide light.

MUTABLE SIGN: Gemini, Virgo, Sagittarius, and Pisces are mutable signs. These signs have a flexible nature and can easily adapt to new situations. They are the "finishers" of the zodiac, as they refine what others have started or built.

NATAL CHART: Also called birth chart. A map of the sky that denotes the position of the planets and other celestial bodies at the time a person was born, based on the exact date, moment, and place of birth. This astrological profile can be interpreted for greater understanding of one's personality and potential.

OUTER PLANET: A planet with an orbit outside the asteroid belt; these planets are farther from the sun and have an indirect effect on personality. Outer planets include Jupiter, Saturn, Uranus, Neptune, and Pluto; these are said to shape generations more than individuals.

PEREGRINE: The state of a planet when it possesses no essential dignity (domicile, exaltation, detriment, or fall). This is a neutral position, in which the planet's energy is neither strengthened nor weakened.

PERSONAL PLANET: See *Inner planet.*

QUALITY: Also known as a modality. Each sign is associated with one of three qualities: cardinal, fixed, or mutable. Each quality dictates a sign's basic approach to life in either controlling (cardinal), sustaining (fixed), or flowing (mutable) with their environment.

RISING SIGN: See *Ascendant.*

RULERSHIP: Strong influence; each sign is ruled by a planet that exerts such influence over it. When a planet is positioned in the sign that it rules over, the planet is said to be in its rulership.

TRANSIT: The passage of a planet or celestial body relative to the location of another celestial body or sector in an astrological chart.

WATER SIGN: Cancer, Scorpio, and Pisces are water signs; they are characterized by emotion and intuition.

CREDITS

SS: Shutterstock, SU: Stocksy United, IS: iStock
Cover and endsheets: Micah Schmidt; All illustrations: Shutterstock

2, Maija Luomala/SS; 4, Jessica Lia/SU; 20, Kara Riley/SU; 22, 134, 192, Alicia Bock/SU; 25, Coldmoon_photo/IS; 27, 36, 55, 97, 106, 181, Coldmoon Photoproject/SS; 29, Epitavi/IS; 34, Franco Antonio Giovanella/Unsplash; 39, 41, 78, 85, 109, vvoe/SS; 43, Bjoern Wylezich/SS; 48, Nadine Greeff/SU; 50, bjphotographs/SS; 53, 169, Roy Palmer/SS; 57, 113, Jiri Vaclavek/SS; 62, Jamie Grill Atlas/SU; 64, 120, Mark Windom/SU; 67, 151, J. Palys/SS; 69, 111, Delennyk/SS; 71, TR_Studio/SS; 76, 118, Micah Schmidt; 81, 83, olpo/SS; 90, 132, Lyuba Burakova/SU; 92, assistant/SS; 95, KrimKate/SS; 99, 127, 148, Cagla Acikgoz/SS; 104, 146, Amber Shumake; 123, Masianya/SS; 125, Nastya22/SS; 137, lermannika/IS; ArgenLant/SS; 141, VvoeVale/IS; 153, Tycson1/SS; 155, Only Fabrizio/SS; 160, Luke SW/SS; 162, ZlataMarka/SS; 165, elen_studio/SS; 167, PHOTO FUN/SS; 174, Catherine MacBride/SU; 176, Erika Kirkpatrick/SS; 179, andy koehler/Adobe Stock; 183, Epitavi/SS; 188, DrPAS/IS